LINCOLN

As I Knew Him

Also by Harold Holzer

———◆◆◆◆———

The Lincoln Image: Abraham Lincoln and the Popular Print
(with Mark E. Neely, Jr., and Gabor S. Boritt)

Changing the Lincoln Image
(with Mark E. Neely, Jr., and Gabor S. Boritt)

The Confederate Image: Prints of the Lost Cause
(with Mark E. Neely, Jr., and Gabor S. Boritt)

Lincoln on Democracy
(with Mario M. Cuomo)

The Lincoln Family Album
(with Mark E. Neely, Jr.)

The Lincoln-Douglas Debates: The First Complete, Unexpurgated Text

Washington and Lincoln Portrayed: National Icons in Popular Prints

Mine Eyes Have Seen the Glory: The Civil War in Art
(with Mark E. Neely, Jr.)

Dear Mr. Lincoln: Letters to the President

Witness to War: The Civil War

The Civil War Era (for young readers)

The Lincoln Mailbag: America Writes to the President

*The Union Preserved: A Guide to Civil War Records
in the New York State Archives*
(with Daniel Lorello)

The Lincoln Forum: Lincoln, Gettysburg, and the Civil War
(with John Y. Simon and William D. Pederson)

LINCOLN
As I Knew Him

GOSSIP, TRIBUTES,
AND REVELATIONS
FROM HIS BEST
FRIENDS AND
WORST ENEMIES

Edited by
HAROLD HOLZER

ALGONQUIN BOOKS
OF CHAPEL HILL
1999

Published by
ALGONQUIN BOOKS OF CHAPEL HILL
Post Office Box 2225
Chapel Hill, North Carolina 27515-2225

a division of
Workman Publishing
708 Broadway
New York, New York 10003

For permission to use photographs and illustrations,
grateful acknowledgment is made to the collection holders,
artists, or representatives named on page 263, which
constitutes an extension of the copyright page.

Library of Congress Cataloging-in-Publication Data
Lincoln as I knew him : gossip, tributes, and
revelations from his best friends and worst enemies /
edited by Harold Holzer.
p.   cm.
Includes bibliographical references (p.   ) and index.
ISBN 1-56512-166-X
1. Lincoln, Abraham, 1809–1865 Anecdotes.
2. Presidents—United States Biography Anecdotes.
3. Lincoln, Abraham, 1809–1865—Friends and associates
Anecdotes.   I. Holzer, Harold.
E457.15 .L53   1999
973.7'092—dc21

[B]

99-23450
CIP

10 9 8 7 6 5 4 3 2 1
First Edition

For Sam Waterston,
who also knows Lincoln

CONTENTS

"WE CANNOT ESCAPE HISTORY.
WE . . . WILL BE REMEMBERED
IN SPITE OF OURSELVES.
NO PERSONAL SIGNIFICANCE, OR
INSIGNIFICANCE, CAN SPARE ONE
OR ANOTHER OF US. THE FIERY
TRIAL THROUGH WHICH WE PASS,
WILL LIGHT US DOWN, IN HONOR
OR DISHONOR, TO THE LATEST
GENERATION."

—ABRAHAM LINCOLN
*from his annual message to Congress,
December 1, 1862*

LINCOLN
As I Knew Him

INTRODUCTION
A GRAND COMPOSITE PICTURE

Abraham Lincoln is at once the most familiar and the most elusive of American heroes.

As much as we know about him—and he has already inspired more books than any figure in our history—he remains fundamentally enigmatic: the quintessential common man possessed of uncommon intellect; the ill-educated child who became the greatest writer among American presidents; the so-called simple country lawyer who rose to the heights of the legal profession in his state; the supposedly awkward public speaker who somehow enthralled most of the audiences that he addressed; the resolute commander in chief who tolerated hundreds of thousands of American casualties in war, yet also revealed a tender heart as likely to pardon as to punish. Such contradictions have fascinated writers and readers alike for more than a century and a quarter. They still do.

Fueling the image of Lincoln as the perennial man of mystery is the absence of surviving revelation from Lincoln himself. "The most reticent, secretive man I ever saw," in the words of his longtime law partner, William H. Herndon, Lincoln disclosed as little about himself as he could, and to as few confidants as possible. Even those who knew him best admitted that he allowed them only brief glimpses into his deepest thoughts and aspirations.[1]

What is more, to the frustration of all historians who have grappled with his life since, Lincoln kept no diary or journal himself. Nor did he live to write a memoir or an autobiography—save for two brief sketches of his first fifty years, cautiously composed for adaptation by campaign biographers in the months leading up to the presidential election of 1860. As deeply as scholars have probed other archives, the only unquestionable biographical sources remain Lincoln's own speeches and letters. Such documents tell us what he believed, but not really what he was like. Where, then, can one search for, let alone discover, the authentic Abraham Lincoln?

Some of the most valuable clues can be found within the personal recollections of Lincoln's contemporaries, rarely mined since, except by professional historians. Written by men and women who knew and observed Lincoln firsthand, these anecdotes and impressions take us as close as we are ever likely to get to the man as he appeared at crucial points of his storied life: during his impoverished childhood; his struggles as a young pioneer in a tiny Illinois village; his arduous life as a peripatetic attorney on the prairie judicial circuit; his emergence in statewide politics; his rise to national prominence; and his stormy tenure in the White House.

Lincoln was vividly remembered by his contemporaries for two important reasons. First—and this should never be forgotten by the astute reader—because he *later* became so famous. As the subject's reputation grew, especially after his assassination and martyrdom, even those with the most fleeting acquaintance came forward with Lincoln memories to share, not all of them enlightening, or even accurate. Audience hunger for such stories nourished a thriving industry of Lincoln reminiscence whose products, some written long after the fact, were not always entirely reliable.

Yet even the most cynical modern auditor of such materials must concede as well that Lincoln was also undeniably memorable, almost from the very start of his life. He seemed, from the beginning, a unique result of environment, natural gifts, and self-discipline, somehow bigger than his milieu, if not always aware of how high he could aspire. His extraordinary appearance, his passionate love of books, great physical strength, incorruptible honesty, skill at debate, tireless quest for political advancement, and the rollicking sense of humor concealing a deep and sometimes debilitating melancholy all made onlookers take early and sustained interest. The man was different. People noticed him. They laughed at his jokes, tried in turn to cheer him when he grew gloomy, marveled at his skills in court and debate, fell under his spell politically. And of course, they remembered.

Relatives who saw him moments after his birth, villagers who heard him speak on the backwoods political stump, functionaries who worked near his side at the White House, foreign and domestic journalists who interviewed him, and political and military leaders who served him during the Civil War all proved after Lincoln's death to be both eager and able—in response to an insatiable public appetite for such insights—to look back to their encounters with the great man and recall them in considerable detail. Some of these intimates might have embellished, others perhaps invented, some specifics. But there could be no doubt that this extraordinarily accessible President also inspired a trove of indelible, irrefutable memories. As a foreign correspondent who visited Washington during the war marveled, Lincoln was "unrestrained in the presence of strangers to a degree perfectly astonishing." Among his friends and associates, notwithstanding the wall of mystery that always seemed to veil him, he was more open still. Lincoln recollectors invariably had much to recall, and much to share.

And their recollections are worth reassessing today. Without them we cannot hope to understand, let alone emulate, the man consistently ranked by professional historians as our greatest president.[2]

These contemporary observations—from the most fleeting to the most sustained—have always been considered prime sources of original material about Lincoln's life and times. Many of the quotes from these eyewitnesses are still cited in biography and history. More often than not, however, the same brief lines are endlessly repeated, merely to be surrounded, in each successive application, by revised interpretation. No systematic effort has been made for several generations to go back to the sources themselves, reevaluate them, and present undistilled the best and most revealing—praiseworthy and critical alike.

The original period reminiscences from which this collection draws first saw light in a variety of forms: letters, diary entries, sermons, lectures, articles, and books. Some of Lincoln's contemporaries, like law partner Herndon and private secretaries John G. Nicolay and John Hay, wrote important biographical studies based on their peerless personal experience and insight. And these particular men did not rely solely on their own memories. They undertook thorough research, conducting extensive interviews with others and soliciting detailed letters about Lincoln from his contemporaries. Some of this data, too, survives, and it, as well as the published books, constitute a priceless lode of recollection.[3]

Other men of Lincoln's era wrote autobiographies that include revealing descriptions of encounters with or impressions of the President. Still others managed modest articles for newspapers and magazines, or contributed their memories to postassassination tribute books and early Lincoln anthologies. Such titles as *Reminiscences of Abraham Lincoln by Distinguished Men of His Time* and *Abraham Lincoln: Tributes from His Associates* abounded in nineteenth-century America, although they have been largely forgotten in decades since, except by scholars.[4]

One project, undertaken in 1895 by *The Independent,* later published as a book, was touted as "a portfolio of . . . vivid and striking snap-shots by men on whose memory some single interview had impressed itself as a great event in their lives. . . ." Together, its editors asserted, such recollections constituted "a grand composite picture, the separate parts all blending into one harmonious whole" and supplying a "many sided view of the man."[5]

Critics of the day applauded such books. The *New York Age* called *The Independent* collection "one of the ablest and most thorough treatments of the subject ever made." And the *Hartford Seminary Record* admitted, "we have found no place where the character of the man himself has been more vividly portrayed than in these reminiscent sketches by men who were associated with him."[6]

Once the "men who were associated with him" died, however—along with the small but important number of women who had also recorded their Lincoln impressions—the fashion for tribute books died, too. Gone was the immediacy of contemporary reminiscence, the hope of tapping one more well of information from someone who had seen and talked to the President. While historians have continued to use such sources in researching their own interpretive works, the fashion for popular editions of collected reminiscences evaporated. Their variety and authentic flavor strongly suggest that their fall from grace was premature and undeserved.[7]

This book represents an attempt to rescue and revive the form—and it seeks to show how Lincoln impressed, and occasionally distressed, a wide variety of observers. It will show how different categories of contemporaries often held wildly varying ideas about this complex man (no small number of them insisting, for example, that the President, so renowned in his own time for enjoying jokes, was actually the gravest of men and never once told a funny story in their presence). And the collection will show, too, how other Lincolnian characteristics — self-assurance, lack of pretense, gloominess, along with his perfectly flabbergasting personal looks — seemed nearly always to strike observers of all kinds. Finally, the collection strives to open a larger window onto the culture of the mid–nineteenth century through the eyes of observers ranging from prairie pioneers to statesmen to leaders of the increasingly impatient African-American population — through whose prism of memory much of Lincoln fact and legend have filtered down to us.

I have spent years combing the archives of public and private collections alike in search of the most illuminating reminiscences. Through them I have seen emerging before my eyes a more complex character than the hero of national myth: a man of both moral principle and political craft, a mirth-provoking companion as well as a superior intellect who read more widely than most biographers have acknowledged; a man of reticence and humor, determination and tenderness, courage and fallibility — and perhaps, most important of all, a man of inexhaustible energy and robust health who could or would not bend to the overwhelming pressure and fatigue of his responsibilities during the Civil War. Weaker people (his own son included) fell victim to Washington's merciless heat and rampant disease, and not much farther south, toil and worry effectively broke the health and spirit of Lincoln's Confederate counterpart, Jefferson Davis. But Abraham Lincoln, as some of these stories attest, never succumbed.

Here are recollections of meetings, trips, court cases, and portrait sittings; reminiscences of speeches, conversations, debates, anecdotes, and feats of strength; and frank, not always flattering assessments of Lincoln's abilities, especially at the outset of his presidential administration. (It must be conceded, however, that sainthood does not provide fertile ground for sowing the seeds of negativity: precious few contemporaries, not even archenemy Jefferson Davis, produced anti-Lincoln reminiscences once the man had been replaced by the myth.) Here instead are the equally important, simple stories by those who had shared Lincoln's youth and marveled at his love of reading and public speaking. And here are the admissions by the most learned men of his age that Lincoln, in the end, seemed to know more than they did.

Admittedly, research made it clear as well that an *over*abundance of recollective material had appeared in print during the golden age of Lincoln literature between 1865 and 1909. Some of it was so obscure it suggested scant reason for exhumation. One example that sticks indelibly in my mind is entitled "Philadelphia Hair Cutter Attended the Great Statesman, and Is Known as 'Lincoln's Little Barber.'" This undated press clipping from the files of the Lincoln Museum in Fort Wayne, Indiana, proved amusing to read, but not exactly worthy of inclusion here. Thus the process of gathering material for this book became one of selectivity as much as discovery.

Recollections must also pass the test of authenticity and they are understandably regarded as decreasingly reliable the longer it takes their writers to commit them to paper. Inarguably, the most dependable reminiscences were written hours, days, or weeks after they were experienced. Recollections written just after Lincoln died, when the marketplace for such accounts abounded with firsthand memories, boast strong value as well, regardless of the competitive atmosphere in which they were introduced. And we should not forget that even the later reminiscences that appeared in the 1870s, 1880s, and 1890s were not immune from the scrutiny of fellow witnesses, still living, who had also observed Lincoln from life and might easily have contradicted the grossest inaccuracy or hyperbole. As for the young children who had glimpsed Lincoln in the 1850s and 1860s and then were prevailed upon in the 1920s and 1930s to reawaken memories going back three quarters of a century, their memories must of course be regarded more dubiously, though one is sorely tempted to allow these last surviving witnesses to speak again from the heart. In the end, this collection allows all the generations of eyewitnesses to come forward once again. Prefaces to each recollection place them within the continuum of the Lincoln reminiscence tradition and evaluate them for dependability.

Early on in this effort, I became convinced that readers would also best be served not only by the most reliable glimpses into Lincoln's appearance, habits, and character, but also by the most vividly reported. So my goal has been to assemble not just the recollections of the people closest to Lincoln (his wife, his son, and his closest legal and political associates, for example), but also the observations of the keenest literary craftsmen of the era, whose powers of analysis and composition can more than make up for the brevity of their exposure to Lincoln. Thus, to a roster that includes the haltingly expressed anecdotes of Lincoln's aged and illiterate stepmother, as told to an interviewer, I have added excerpts from original articles written by Harriet Beecher Stowe and Nathaniel Hawthorne. These writers enjoyed interviews with Lincoln during the war and went on to write eloquently about him in pieces that have seldom been reprinted in any substantial form since their initial appearance in the nineteenth century.

The other "contributors" to this collection range from family members to political associates, from the celebrated political and military leaders of Lincoln's own time to aides who worked for or near him during the rebellion: a clerk, a bodyguard, a telegraph operator, even his sons' baby-sitter. The great African-American leader Frederick Douglass speaks again about the "white man's president" who nonetheless treated him as a brother. Poet Walt Whitman weaves vivid impressions from a chance encounter, a glance, and a smile, into an evocatively imagined friendship. A cabinet minister recalls the day Lincoln announced the momentous Emancipation Proclamation — preceding it with a comic reading from one of his favorite humorists. And the humorist himself observes Lincoln through the lens of bravura, if folksy, comedy. An artist sketches him; a sculptor models his bust. Observers laugh with him, try (and mostly fail) to penetrate his distracted personality, and take stock of his wholly original, truly remarkable appearance. The long out of print, the seldom published, the inexplicably neglected, and the vexingly condensed have all been called back to life.

Few observers take stock of a Lincolnian trait that should be acknowledged at the outset: he was not a particularly faithful friend. He had a great concern "for the people," but maybe not so much for *people*. With an ambition as furiously stoked as an "engine," as his law partner admitted, he attracted loyal followers, but had little time for intimacy. So, once he moved from his parents' cabin to New Salem, he all but cut himself off from his family. Once in Springfield, he had little to do with his New Salem acquaintances. And in the White House, he disappointed many old Springfield supporters by failing to provide them with the government jobs to which they aspired. When Abraham Lincoln moved on, he tended to leave old friends behind. But if he forgot his old friends, at least they did not forget *him,* as these memories will confirm.

I would be less than candid if I did not concede that the resulting anthology unapologetically reflects on occasion my own preferences and prejudices. I cheerfully admit an incurable affection for passages from certain contemporary accounts that have long given me pleasure and insight and that I felt could not possibly be excluded from such a collection. I can only hope that these texts now evoke similar appreciation from others.

Ideally, the sum and substance of the result—though representing barely a taste of the truly staggering weight of recollected material inspired by the outpouring of postassassination Lincoln reverence—will bring readers a bit closer to the Lincoln who walked, spoke, laughed, and led, and was the flesh-and-blood contemporary of a now long-gone generation of witnesses.

In one sense, their accounts constitute a collective biography. But in another sense, Lincoln will likely emerge yet again as an irresistible paradox, as familiar as the engraving on the ubiquitous copper penny, as remote as the godlike figure enthroned in the Lincoln Memorial. He remains so accessible that we embrace him, yet so distant that we yearn to know him better. Hopefully, this freshly assembled material will take us another step closer to Lincoln. For to understand Lincoln is to comprehend America itself—the democracy he symbolized with his rise and sanctified with his leadership.

1. MEMORIES FROM FAMILY

———◆———

Lincoln had not one but three families: those of his natural parents, of his stepmother, and finally of his wife. But when he opened the door to include the last, he closed it on the first two. Where family was concerned, Lincoln proved a man of scant sentiment.

The exceptions were his own children. Lincoln was a loving and tolerant father to his four sons, happily allowing them to run wild in public (see the sour recollections of such permissiveness from his law partner William H. Herndon).

Yet he harbored little of the same pride when it came to his prairie forebears. His chilly relationship with his father (he refused the elder Lincoln's last entreaties to visit his deathbed), acknowledged in the memories of his stepmother, may have been the rule, not the exception. For though he adored his father's second wife, Lincoln seems to have been ungenerous in providing for her in her later years. And when his stepbrother John D. Johnston came to him once, desperate for money, Lincoln called him "an *idler*" and sternly advised him to get a job.

Most astounding of all, Lincoln never introduced his stepmother to his own wife or children. She never met them. Writing to the old lady—probably for the first time ever—after her husband's assassination, Mary Lincoln had to tell her mother-in-law that grandchild Thomas, also known as "Tad," had been named for the late President's father. Mary believed that Sarah did not know this elementary family fact, a none too flattering comment on Lincoln as a son.

Lincoln proved far kinder to Mary's relatives—particularly when it came to dispensing presidential patronage to assorted Todds—than he was to the Lincoln, Hanks (his natural mother's clan), and Johnston families. In marrying, Lincoln moved up in the world and thereafter he avoided looking back to the poverty-stricken prairie relations whom he had left behind. Lincoln never even paid to have a headstone erected over his father's grave.

In the following reminiscences, his stepmother, country cousins, wife, and young son all share intimate memories of Lincoln. Lincoln revealed little of himself to later acquaintances. These people knew him earliest, and probably best. ⁑

"Abe Was the Best Boy I Ever Saw"

SARAH BUSH JOHNSTON LINCOLN

1788–1869
STEPMOTHER

Following the untimely death of Abraham Lincoln's mother, his father, Thomas, remarried. His bride was Sarah Bush Johnston, a widow with three children of her own, "a poor woman," a contemporary remembered, "but of spotless character." Sally, as she was called, took an immediate liking to Abraham, and by all accounts the feeling was mutual. She encouraged her stepson to read and study; all of the boy's "early training," an old friend recalled, came "under this good woman."

In later years, though he distanced himself from his father, Lincoln visited his stepmother in her primitive cabin when the law or politics took him to the old neighborhood, and occasionally he provided money to help support her. Their last visit, shortly after the presidential election of 1860, was, an eyewitness testified, emotional. Lincoln was "very kind to his step mother who embraced and cried over him." Yet there was a limit to their bond: Lincoln never introduced Sarah to his wife and sons.

Five months after Lincoln's assassination, his former law partner, William H. Herndon, contemplating a biography of his famous friend, journeyed to "Old Mrs. Lincoln's Home," as he noted, "9 m South of Charleston," Illinois, to interview the woman who knew the boy Lincoln best. Sally was then around seventy-seven years old. ✛

A BE WAS ABOUT 9 YEARS OF AGE WHEN I LANDED IN INDIANA. THE COUNTRY WAS WILD AND DESOLATE. ABE WAS A GOOD BOY: HE DIDN'T LIKE PHYSICAL LABOR—WAS DILIGENT FOR knowledge—wished to know and if pains and labor would get it he was sure to get it. He was the best boy I ever saw. He read all the books he could lay his hands on—I can't remember dates nor names— am about 75 years of age. Abe read the bible some, though not as much as said: he sought more congenial books—suitable for his age. I think newspapers were had in Indiana as early as 1824 and up to 1830 when we moved to Illinois. Abe was a constant reader of them—I am sure of this for the years of 1827–28–29–30. The name of the Louisville Journal seems to sound like one [unlikely, as it began publication after Lincoln left home—ed.]. Abe read histories, papers, and other books—can't name any one—have forgotten. Abe had no particular religion—didn't think of that question at that time, if he ever did. He never talked about it. He read diligently—studied in the day time—didn't after night much—went to bed early—got up early and then read—eat his breakfast—go to work in the field with the men. Abe read all the books he could lay his hands on—and when he came across a passage that struck him he would write it down on boards if he had no paper and keep it there till he did get paper—then he would re-write it—look at, it repeat it. He had a copy book—a kind of scrap book in which he put down all things and this preserved them. He ciphered on boards when he had no paper or no slate and when the board would get too black he would shave it off with a drawing knife and go on again: When he had paper he put his sums down on it. His copy book is here now or was lately. Abe, when old folks were at our house, was a silent and attentive observer—never speaking or asking questions till they were gone and then he must understand everything—even to the smallest thing—minutely and exactly. He would then repeat it over to himself again and again—sometimes in one form and then in another and when it was fixed in his mind to suit him he became easy and he never lost that fact or his understanding of it. Sometimes he seemed pestered to give expression to his ideas and got mad almost at one who couldn't explain plainly what he wanted to convey. He would hear sermons preached—come home—take the children out—get on a stump or log and almost repeat it word for word. He made other speeches such as interested him and the children. His father had to make him quit sometimes as he quit his own work to speak and made the other children as well as the men quit their work. As a usual thing Mr. Lincoln never made Abe quit reading to do anything if he could avoid it. He would do it himself first. Mr. Lincoln could read a little and could scarcely write his name: hence he wanted, as he himself felt the uses and necessities of education his boy

Abraham to learn and he encouraged him to do it in all ways he could —Abe was a poor boy, and I can say what scarcely one woman—a mother—can say in a thousand and it is this—Abe never gave me a cross word or look and never refused in fact, or even in appearance, to do any thing I requested him. I never gave him a cross word in all my life. He was kind to everybody and to everything and always accommodated others if he could—would do so willingly if he could. His mind and mine—what little I had—seemed to run together—move in the same channel. Abe could easily learn and long remember and when he did learn anything he learned it well and thoroughly. What he thus learned he stowed away in his memory which was extremely good. What he learned and stowed away was well defined in his own mind—repeated over and over again and again till it was so defined and fixed firmly and permanently in his memory. He rose early—went to bed early, not reading much after night. Abe was a moderate eater and I now have no remembrance of his special dish: he sat down and ate what was set before him, making no complaint: he seemed careless about this. I cooked his meals for nearly 15 years. He always had good health—never was sick—was very careful of his person—was tolerably neat and clean only—cared nothing for clothes—so that they were clean and neat—fashion cut no figure with him—nor color—nor stuff nor material—was careless about these things. He was more fleshy in Indiana than ever in Illinois. I saw him every year or two—he was here—after he was elected President of the U.S. (Here the old lady stopped—turned around and cried—wiped her eyes—and proceeded.)

As company would come to our house Abe was a silent listener—wouldn't speak—would sometimes take a book and retire aloft—go to the stable or field or woods—and read. Abe was always fond of fun—sport—wit and jokes. He was sometimes very witty indeed. He never drank whiskey or other strong drink—was temperate in all things—too much so I thought sometimes. He never told me a lie in his life—never evaded—never equivocated never dodged—nor turned a corner to avoid any chastisment or other responsibility. He never swore or used profane language in my presence nor in others that I now remember of. He duly reverenced old age—loved those best about his own age—played with those under his age. He listened to the aged—argued with his equals—but played with the children. He loved animals generally and treated them kindly: he loved children well, very well. There seemed to be nothing unusual in his love for animals or his own kind—though he treated everybody and everything kindly—humanely—Abe didn't care much for crowds of people: he choose his own company which was always good. He was not very fond of girls as he seemed to me. He sometimes attended church. He would repeat the sermon over again to the children. The sight of such a thing amused all and did especially tickle the children. When Abe was reading my husband took particular care not to disturb him—would let him read on and on till Abe quit of his own accord. He was dutiful to me always—he loved me truly I think. I had a son John who was raised with Abe. Both were good boys, but I must say—both now being dead that Abe was the best boy I ever saw or ever expect to see. I wish

I had died when my husband died. I did not want Abe to run for President—did not want him elected—was afraid somehow or other—felt it in my heart that something would happen [to] him and when he came down to see me after he was elected President I still felt that something told me that something would befall Abe and that I should see him no more. Abe and his father are in Heaven I have no doubt, and I want to go there—go where they are. God bless Abraham.

"Hungry for Books"

DENNIS HANKS
(1799–1893)
COUSIN

No one knew Lincoln better in his youth—or lived longer and told more tales about their hard life together as boys on the frontier—than this incorrigible first cousin of Lincoln's mother. Ten years older and a close neighbor, Dennis was Abe's mentor on the prairie and doubtless taught him much (he even claimed he "taught Abe to write with a buzzard's quillen which I killed with a rifle & having made a pen, put Abe's hand in mind & moving his fingers by my hand to give him the idea of how to write"). When Lincoln's mother, along with Hanks's guardians, died during an 1818 epidemic in Indiana, Dennis moved into the Lincoln family cabin, living with them for three years—sometimes observing what his stepmother failed to recollect—until he married Abraham's stepsister. He moved on to Illinois with the family in 1830, after which Lincoln seldom saw him.

Years later, Dennis surprised President Lincoln with an unannounced visit to the White House. Lincoln gave the old man a watch chain and heard his report about a recent anti-draft riot in their old Charleston, Illinois, neighborhood. Dennis had been dispatched to win his cousin's support for pardoning the rioters. Dennis lived for decades on his colorful Lincoln stories. He died in his ninety-fourth year—only after being knocked down by a carriage after yet another public Lincoln event at which he had doubtless spun his yarns.

The following reminiscence is excerpted from a June 1865 letter Hanks wrote to Lincoln's former law partner, William H. Herndon, who requested it for his proposed biography of the late President. ✦

ABE WAS A GOOD BOY—AN AFFECTIONATE ONE—A BOY WHO LOVED HIS FATHER AND MOTHER DEARLY AND WELL, ALWAYS MINDING THEM WELL—SOMETIMES ABE WAS A LITTLE RUDE. When strangers would ride along and up to his father's fence Abe always, through pride and to tease his father, would be sure to ask the stranger the first question, for which his father would sometimes knock him a rod. Abe was then a rude and forward boy. Abe when whipped by his father, never bawled but dropt a kind of silent unwelcome tear, as evidence of his sensations—or other feelings. . . .

. . . Abe was getting hungry for books, reading everything he could lay his hands on. The marriage of Thomas Lincoln and the widow Johnson [Sarah Bush Johnston—ed.] was in 1821—Abraham being now 12 years old. Webster's old Spelling Book—the life [of] Henry Clay—Robinson Crusoe—Weems Life of Washington—*Aesops*

Fables—Bunyan's *Pilgrim's Progress*—I do not say that Lincoln read these books just then but he did between this time [1821—ed.] and 1825. He was a constant and I may say stubborn reader, his father having sometimes to slash him for neglecting his work by reading. Mr. Lincoln—Abe's father—often said I had to pull the old sow up to the trough—when speaking of Abe's reading and how he got to it, then and how he had to pull her away. . . .

. . . About the year 1825 or 1826, Abe borrowed of [neighbor] Josiah Crawford Ramsay's Life of Washington—which got spoiled as specified generally in the Presidents life [it was damaged in a rainstorm—ed.] and paid as therein described. He pulled fodder at 25 cents per day to pay for it. He worked three or four days. Abe was then growing to be a man and about 15 or 16 years of age. He was then just the same boy in every particular that he subsequently exhibited to the world from 1831—to the time of his death. At this early age he was more humorous than in after life—full of fun—wit—humor, and if he ever got a new story, new book or new fact or idea, he never forgot it. He was honest—faithful—loving truth, speaking it at all times—and never flinching therefrom. Physically he was a stout and powerful boy—fat, round, plump and well made as well as proportioned. This continued to be so up to the time he landed in [New] Salem, Sangamon County. In 1825 or 1826 he then exhibited a love for poetry and wrote a piece of humorous rhyme on his friend Josiah Crawford that made all the neighbors Crawford included burst their sides with laughter. I had it was lost in the fire. He was humorous funny—witty and good humored in all times. . . .

. . . It must have been about this time that Abe got kicked by a horse in the mill and who did not speak for several hours and when he did speak—he ended the sentence which he commenced to the horse as I am well informed and believe. From this last period, 1825–6 & 7, Lincoln was constantly reading, writing—cipher a little in Pikes Arithmetic. He excelled any boy I ever saw, putting his opportunities into conversation. . . . Truth and justice—and mankind will make him the great of the world. He needs no fictions to back him. Lincoln sometimes attempted to sing but always failed, but while this is true he was harmony and time—and sound. He loved such music as he knew the words of. He was a tricky man and sometimes when he went to log house raising—corn shucking and such like things, he would say to himself and sometimes to others—I don't want these fellows to work any more and instantly he would commence his pranks—tricks—jokes—stories—and sure enough all would stop—gather around Abe and listen, sometimes crying—and sometimes bursting their sides with laughter. He sometimes would mount a stump—chair or box and make speeches—speech with stories—anecdotes and such like thing. He never failed here. At this time Abe was . . . as before a kind of forward boy and sometimes forward too when he got stubborn. His nature went an entire revolution. One thing is true of him—always was up to 1830, when our intimacy ended, because he went to Sangamon and I went to Coles Co. He was ambitious and determined and when he attempted to excel by man or boy his whole soul and his energies were bent on doing it—and he in this generally—almost always accomplished his ends.

"He Was Not a Brilliant Boy"

JOHN HANKS
(1802–1889)
COUSIN

Another cousin on his mother's side, John resided with the Lincoln family in their Indiana cabin for four years—chopping wood, building log fences, and working the fields on Thomas Lincoln's farm alongside the future president.

In 1831 Hanks and Lincoln piloted a flatboat down the Mississippi to New Orleans, where Lincoln saw his first slave market. The two cousins were for a time quite close.

It was Hanks who, in 1860, entered an Illinois political meeting toting log rails that he boasted had been split by the young Lincoln. The relics helped fuel the image of Lincoln, the self-made "Railsplitter," whose extraordinary rise from poverty and obscurity became the talk of the presidential campaign.

The following recollection comes from his remarks to William H. Herndon in June 1865. The illiterate Hanks "authenticated" it with his mark—an "X." ✣

ABRAHAM WAS KNOWN AMONG THE BOYS AS A BASHFUL SOMEWHAT DULL, BUT PEACEABLE BOY. HE WAS NOT A BRILLIANT BOY, BUT WORKED HIS WAY BY TOIL. TO LEARN WAS HARD FOR him, but he walked slowly, but surely. . . .

When Lincoln, Abe and I, returned to the house from work, he would go to the cupboard, snatch a piece of corn bread, take down a book, sit down on a chair, cock his legs up as high as his head, and read. He and I worked barefooted—grubbed it, plowed, mowed, and cradled together, plowed corn, gathered and shucked corn. Abraham read constantly when he had an opportunity—no newspapers then. . . . I know he read Weems' [Life of] Washington when I was there—got it wet. It was on a kind of book shelf close to the window. The book shelf was made by two pins in the wall and a clap board on them, books on that. Lincoln got it of [Josiah] Crawford [a neighbor, ed.], told Crawford and paid it in pulling fodder by two or three days' work. He frequently read the Bible. He read *Robinson Crusoe,* Bunyan's *Pilgrim's Progress.* Lincoln devoured all the books he could get or lay hands on: he was a constant and voracious reader.

I never could get him in company with women: he was not a timid man in this particular, but did not seek such company. He was always full of his stories. . . . He would go out in the woods and gather hickory bark, bring it home and keep a light by it and read by it, when no lamp was to be had—grease lamp—handle to it which stuck in the crack of the wall. Tallow was scarce.

Abraham was a good and hearty eater—loved good eating. His own mother and stepmother were good cooks for them days and times. In the summer he wore tow linen pants and flax shirt and in the winter he wore linsey woolsey [a coarse blend of linen and wool—ed.]—that is, during the time I was there. I have seen Lincoln—Abe—make speeches to his stepbrothers—stepsisters—and youngsters that would come to see the family.

"The Depth, Tenderness, and Purity of Mr. Lincoln's Nature"

ELIZABETH TODD GRIMSLEY

(1825–1895)

COUSIN-IN-LAW

"Lizzie" was Mary's cousin and a bridesmaid at the Lincoln wedding. Mary referred to her as a "noble, good woman," and remained close to her throughout her life. In 1861, Mrs. Grimsley accompanied the Lincolns from Illinois to Washington and stayed with the family for six months, helping the new First Lady set up housekeeping in the badly neglected White House.

Barely a month into her residence, however, Mary's cousin began campaigning for a federal job—that of postmaster of Springfield—only to be rejected by the President. She sought the job again in 1864, writing directly to Lincoln in the hope that his original objection—"that a Post-Mistress in a place the size of Springfield would produce a dis-satisfaction"—would no longer prevail, but again he turned her down.

If she harbored any bitterness, however, it did not surface in her memoir, published many years later, of her half year in Washington.

The following glimpse into White House family life is taken from that recollection. ✤

———◆◆◆———

THE REGIMENTS [OF SOLDIERS—ED.] WERE SCATTERED IN DIF-
FERENT PARTS OF WASHINGTON, AND BETWEEN THE WHITE
HOUSE AND THE WAR DEPARTMENT WAS QUITE A LARGE
encampment which had a peculiar charm for our little boys, and Taddie's rollicking ways afforded them quite a diversion. There was nothing in the way of fruit, flowers, books, or papers Tad would withhold
from "his good soldiers," and our visits to the conservatory to which
I had free access, were a frequent source of grief to the caretakers, who
did not relish having their treasures despoiled for men.

One morning, Mr. Lincoln coming in to a late breakfast, (by the
way a most frequent occurrence in these troublous times) found his
"little man" dissolved in tears, a sight he could never serenely bear, and
at once set about to discover the trouble. "Why! Faver [Tad suffered
from a speech impediment and could not pronounce his "th" sound,
ed.], such ungrateful soldiers! When I gave them tracts, and asked
them to read them, they laughed loud at me, and said they had plenty
of paper to start fires with, and would rather have a 'posey.'" His father
took him in his arms, pressed him tightly to him, kissed him, and tried
to console him, but it was days before the men saw their little friend's
laughing face again, as he could not readily forgive ridicule.

Willie [Lincoln's middle son—ed.], who was seated at the table next to Mr. Galloway of Ohio, looked most sorrowfully at Tad during this scene, and then lapsed into a profound, absorbed silence, which Mr. Lincoln would not allow to be disturbed. This lasted ten or fifteen minutes, then he clasped both hands together, shut his teeth firmly over the under lip, and looked up smilingly into his father's face, who exclaimed, "There! you have it now, my boy, have you not?" Turning to Mr. Galloway he said, "I know every step of the process by which that boy arrived at his satisfactory solution of the question before him, as it is by just such slow methods that I attain results."

What the question was, we never knew, save that it was some scheme which he could apply as a balm to Taddie's wounded feelings.

In some of these camp excursions the boys contracted the measles and for two or three weeks were quite sick. The mother, always over-anxious and worried about the boys and withal not a skillful nurse, was totally unfitted for caring for them. They disliked their attendant maid, and by degrees, I was inveigled into the nursery, and by way of a pet name, was dubbed "Grandmother," though a younger woman than the mother.

But I never regretted the days thus spent, for then I learned to know the depth, tenderness, and purity of Mr. Lincoln's nature, his gentleness and patience. "Kind little words, which are of the same blood as great and holy deeds," flowed from his lips constantly to these sick children, the anxious mother, and all others. These were days to be remembered, as this weary over-burdened man found his way through the crowds which still gathered in every hall, to the room where he knew he would bring comfort, and find us with a fragrant cup of tea, and a tempting lunch ready for him. After eating he would stretch himself upon the couch, with a book in his hand, as often the Bible as any other, for he felt there was nothing in literature that would compare with poetic Job, Moses the Law Giver, the beautiful and varied experiences of the Psalms of David, or the grand majestic utterances of Isaiah. He would read aloud to us, recite some poem, until recalled to the cares of state by the messenger. And this was, at that time, the only relaxation he took.

"The Largest One for Father"

WILLIAM WALLACE LINCOLN
(1850–1862)
SON

"Willie" was the Lincoln's third son—and also, recalled a Springfield neighbor, "the favorite, being, like his father, very companionable and democratic in his manner." His tragic death from typhoid at age eleven sent his mother into a period of intense mourning from which she never really recovered.

Willie had been developing into a talented writer. His "first attempt at poetry," as he put it, an ode to the martyred Col. Edward Dickinson Baker, an old family friend, was judged by the editor of the Washington *National Republican* to be "quite creditable, as a first effort, for one so young." The verses were published in that newspaper in 1861. Two years earlier, Willie had written his only lines about his father, in a letter to a friend named Henry Remann. In the note, the child touchingly described a trip the two were sharing to Chicago, where Lincoln was appearing in a legal case. This is how life with his father at the Tremont House appeared to a wide-eyed William Wallace Lincoln on 3 June 1859. ✤

———◆◆◆———

THIS TOWN IS A VERY BEAUTIFUL PLACE. ME AND FATHER WENT TO TWO THEATRES THE OTHER NIGHT. ME AND FATHER HAVE A NICE LITTLE ROOM TO OURSELVES. WE HAVE TWO LITTLE pitcher[s] on a washstand. The smallest one for me the largest one for father. We have two little towels on a top of both pitchers. The smallest one for me, the largest one for father.

We have two little beds in the room. The smallest one for me, the largest one for father.

We have two little wash basin[s]. The smallest one for me, the largest one for father. The weather is very very fine here in this town. Was this exhibition on Wednesday before last.

"My Noble and Good Husband"

MARY LINCOLN

(1818–1882)

WIFE

Lincoln married Mary Todd in November 1842 in Springfield, Illinois, after a rocky courtship that proved the harbinger of a difficult but enduring, and essentially loving, marriage. They could not have been less alike. Mary could be shrewish, pretentious, unreasonable, and sometimes hysterical, tendencies probably accentuated by what later medical parlance might describe as "woman's troubles." Lincoln was distant, unresponsive, moody, and worked endless hours, often traveling away from home half of each year.

Despite long separations and radically different temperaments, the Lincolns remained devoted to each other. Even as President, burdened though he was by disunion and rebellion, Lincoln remained protective of his fragile wife, especially after their son Willie died of typhoid in the White House. As for the First Lady, she maintained a fierce loyalty to the man she referred to, in her correspondence, as "my idolized Husband," or "my sainted husband." If opposites truly attract, notwithstanding tragedies, conflicts, and pressures, then the Lincolns were, in a sense, made for each other.

The first recollection here comes from Mary's letter to artist Francis B. Carpenter, then planning a Lincoln family portrait. The memory was written down exactly seven months after the President's death.

The second selection is excerpted from surviving transcripts of the interview Mary granted William H. Herndon in September 1866, when Lincoln's former law partner was in the early stages of research for his biography—and before Herndon outraged Mary with his assertion that Lincoln had loved only the late Ann Rutledge, not his widow. The notes are in Herndon's hand, unsigned by the widow, but confirm her idealized view of her martyred husband. ✤

HOW I WISH YOU COULD HAVE SEEN MY DEAR HUSBAND THE LAST THREE WEEKS OF HIS LIFE! HAVING A REALIZING SENSE THAT THE UNNATURAL REBELLION WAS NEAR ITS CLOSE, AND being most of the time *away* from Washington, where he had endured such conflicts of mind within the last four years, feeling *so encouraged,* he freely gave vent to his cheerfulness. Down the Potomac [on a trip to visit General Grant in early April 1865—ed.] he was almost boyish in his mirth and reminded me of his original nature, what I had always remembered of him, in our own home—free from care, surrounded by those he loved so well and *by whom* he was so idolized. *The Friday* [of the assassination—ed.], I never saw him so supremely cheerful— his manner was even playful. At three o'clock in the afternoon, he drove out with me in the open carriage. In starting, I asked him if anyone should accompany us. He immediately replied—"No—I prefer to ride by ourselves today." During the drive he was so gay that I said to him, laughingly, "Dear Husband, you almost startle me by your great cheerfulness." He replied, "and well I may feel so, Mary; I consider *this day,* the war has come to a close" and then added, "We must *both* be more cheerful in the future—between the war and the loss of our darling Willie—we have both been very miserable." Every word, then uttered, is deeply engraven on my poor broken heart. In the evening his mind was fixed upon having some relaxation and bent on the theater. Yet I firmly believe that if he had remained at the White House on that night of darkness, when the fiends prevailed, he would have been horribly *cut to pieces.* Those fiends had too long contemplated this inhuman murder to have allowed *him* to escape.

My husband intended when he was through with his Presidential time to take me and family to Europe—didn't in late days dream of death—was cheery, funny, in high spirits. He intended to return and go to California, over the Rocky Mountains, and see the prospect of the soldiers etc. digging out gold to pay the national debt.

He and [Sen. Charles] Sumner were like boys during his last days. Down on the River after Richmond was taken they acted like boys —were so glad the war was over. Mr. Lincoln wanted to live in Springfield and be buried there up to 1865—[then] changed his notion [of] where to live—never settled on any place particularly. . . .

Mr. Lincoln was the kindest, most tenderhearted, and loving husband and father in the world. He gave us all unbounded liberty, said to me always when I asked him for anything: you know what you want—go and get it. He never asked me if it was necessary. He was very, very indulgent to his children—chided or praised for it he always said, "It is my pleasure that my children are free, happy, and unrestrained by parental tyranny. Love is the chain whereby to lock a child to its parent. . . ."

I often said that God would not let any harm come of my husband. We had passed through five long, terrible, bloody years unscathed that I thought so—so did Mr. Lincoln: he was happy over that idea. He was cheerful—almost joyous as he got gradually to see the end of the war.

I used to read newspaper charges—newspaper attacks on him. He said: "Don't do that, for I have enough to bear. Yet I care nothing for them. If I am right, I'll live, and if wrong, I'll die anyhow. So let them pass unnoticed." I would playfully say, "That's the way to learn—read both sides."

Mr. Lincoln's maxim and philosophy was, "What is to be will be and no cares of ours can arrest the decree."

I could tell when Mr. Lincoln had decided anything: he was cheerful at first, then he pressed or compressed his lips tightly and firmly. When these things showed themselves to me, I fashioned myself accordingly and so all others had to do sooner or later—and the world found it out. When we first went to Washington many thought Mr. Lincoln weak. But he rose up grandly with the circumstances and men soon learned that he was above them all. I never saw a man's mind develop so finely. His manners got quite polished.

He used to say to me, when I talked to him about [Secretary of the Treasury Salmon P.] Chase and those who did him evil: "Do good to those who hate you and turn their ill will to friendship." Sometimes in Washington, worn down, he spoke crabbedly to men—yet it seemed that the people understood conditions around him and forgave.

2. MEMORIES FROM PERSONAL
AND POLITICAL FRIENDS

T he better part of one's life," Lincoln wrote in 1849, "consists of his friendships . . ." Yet Lincoln spent the better part of *his* life cultivating a wide net of acquaintances—and only a handful of truly close relationships with friends. As a prominent and ambitious polit-ical leader, he would be called upon to write innumerable letters in-troducing or acknowledging one "very good friend" or another. Ward Hill Lamon, for example, was his "particular friend"; Jesse K. Dubois was "one of his closest and most intimate friends."

But most of them were political supporters who had proven their loyalty, not earned his close confidence. The only true intimate friend of his life was Joshua Fry Speed, with whom he lived in Springfield until he returned to Kentucky to get married. The two men kept up an extremely personal correspondence over the years, and Lincoln later entertained the idea of naming his first son for Speed. But like many of Lincoln's early friendships, this one faded over time.

Yet he managed to convince many of these old and occasionally discarded friends that they knew him well, well enough to enjoy his humor, sympathize with his melancholia, and most important of all, respond to his political leadership—Lincoln's sole loyalty test for prospective "friends." The truth is that he gave of himself to such acquaintances with notorious stinginess.

"He always told me only enough of his plans and purposes to induce the belief that he had communicated all," one old friend recalled. "Yet he reserved enough to have communicated nothing." Maybe Lincoln's friends knew only that part of him that he permitted them to know, but still most recognized that they were experiencing something extraordinary. And they remembered. ✛

"He Had an Immense Stock of Common Sense"

JOSEPH GILLESPIE

(1809–1885)

LONGTIME FRIEND

This fellow Illinois lawyer first met the future President during the Black Hawk War of 1832 and remained a friend, professional colleague, and political ally for three decades. Gillespie studied at Transylvania College and became an attorney and a state legislator. Like Lincoln he was a Whig in politics, later joining the fledgling Republican party in Illinois. Beginning in 1861, he served thirteen years on the circuit bench.

His recollections are drawn from two letters of reminiscences composed in 1866. The "hasty sketch" represented, in the author's own words, "about all I can scrape up relating to Mr. Lincoln." Gillespie was too modest. His insightful observations constitute one of the most valuable of such recollections ever written.

HE WAS GENIAL BUT NOT VERY SOCIABLE. HE DID NOT SEEK COMPANY BUT WHEN HE WAS IN IT HE WAS THE MOST ENTERTAINING PERSON I EVER KNEW. . . .

. . . His love of wealth was very weak. I asked him . . . how much land he owned. He said that the house and lot he lived on and one forty-acre tract was all the real estate he owned and that he got the forty for his services in the Black Hawk War. I inquired why he never speculated in land and pointed to a tract that I had located with a land-warrant which cost me ninety cents an acre. He said he had no capacity whatever for speculation and never attempted it. All the use Mr. Lincoln had for wealth was to enable him to appear respectable. He never hoarded nor wasted but used money as he needed it and gave himself little or no concern about laying up.

He was the most indulgent parent I ever knew. His children literally ran over him and he was powerless to withstand their importunities. He was remarkably tender of the feelings of others and never wantonly offended even the most despicable although he was a man of great nerve when aroused. I have seen him on several occasions display great heroism, when the circumstances seemed to demand it. He was very sensitive where he thought he had failed to come up to the expectations of his friends. I remember a case. He was pitted by the Whigs in 1840 to debate with Mr. Douglas the Democratic champion. Lincoln did not come up to the requirements of the occasion. He was conscious of his failure and I never saw any man so much distressed.

He begged to be permitted to try it again and was reluctantly indulged and in the next effort he transcended our highest expectations. I never heard and never expect to hear such a triumphant vindication as he then gave of Whig measures or policy. He never after to my knowledge fell below himself.

Mr. Lincoln had the appearance of being a slow thinker. My impression is that he was not so slow as he was careful. He never liked to put forth a proposition without revolving it over in his own mind but when he was compelled to act promptly, as in debate, he was quick enough. Douglas, who was a very skillful controversialist, never obtained any advantage over him. I never could discover anything in Mr. Lincoln's mental composition remarkably singular. His qualities were those ordinarily given to mankind but he had them in remarkable degree. He was wonderfully kind, careful, and just. He had an immense stock of common sense and he had faith enough to trust it in every emergency. He had passed through all the grades of society when he reached the Presidency, and he had found common sense a sure reliance and he put it into practice. He acted all through his career upon just such principles as every man of good common sense would approve and say, "that is just as I would have done myself." There was nothing of the Napoleonic in his style of doing things. If he had been in Napoleon's place he never would have gone off to Egypt to strike a blow at England, and he would have been equally careful not to send an army to Moscow. Lincoln had no superhuman qualities (which we call genius) but he had those which belong to mankind generally in an astonishing degree.

There was a tinge of sadness in Mr. Lincoln's composition. He was not naturally disposed to look on the bright side of the picture. He felt very strongly that there was more of discomfort than real happiness in human existence under the most favorable circumstances, and the general current of his reflections was in that channel. He never obtruded these views upon others, but on the contrary strove as much as possible to be gay and lively. There was a slight dash of what is generally called superstition in Mr. Lincoln's mind. He evidently believed that the perceptions were sometimes more unerring than reason and outstripped it. I can't say that he believed in presentiments, but he undoubtedly had gloomy forebodings as to himself. He told me after his election that he did not count confidentially, on living to get through with the task set before him; and I did not think that he apprehended death in the natural way, still I do not believe that he took any precautions to guard against danger. I met him once, coming alone from the war office to the White House, and remarked to him that I thought he was exposing himself to danger of assassination. He replied that no precautions he could take would be availing if they were determined to kill him. I rode out with him that evening to the Soldiers' Home [Lincoln's summer residence—ed.], when he was accompanied by an escort of cavalry; on the way he said that the escort was rather forced upon him by the military men, that he could see no certain protection against assassination if it was determined to take away his life. He said it seemed to him like putting up the gap in only one place when the fence was down all along.

"The Tenderest Heart"

JOSHUA FRY SPEED
(1814–1882)
BEST FRIEND

Speed was the closest friend Lincoln ever had. He took Lincoln into his home when the aspiring lawyer first arrived in Springfield, Illinois, in 1837, and the two shared lodgings, sleeping in the same bed—not uncommon among frugal young men in the nineteenth-century West —for four years. In 1999, a well-known playwright claimed to have uncovered a long-hidden Speed diary containing explosive evidence that the two friends were actually homosexual lovers. The revelations ignited a sensation, but no diary evidence was ever produced, and the notion that Lincoln was, in fact, gay is as unlikely as it is unprovable.

When Speed returned to his native Kentucky and took a wife, he and Lincoln exchanged frank, revealing correspondence on the subject of marriage. Speed's happiness may have been instrumental in convincing a reluctant Lincoln to go through with his own union with Mary Todd in 1842.

Speed and Lincoln ultimately drifted apart, but remained on good terms. As President, Lincoln appointed Speed's brother U.S. attorney general. The following reminiscence comes from a lecture Joshua Speed delivered, published in 1884 as "Reminiscences of Abraham Lincoln." ✣

I T WAS IN THE SPRING OF 1837, AND ON THE VERY DAY THAT HE OBTAINED HIS [LAW] LICENSE, THAT OUR INTIMATE ACQUAINTANCE BEGAN. HE HAD RIDDEN INTO TOWN ON A BORROWED horse, with no earthly property save a pair of saddle-bags containing a few clothes. I was a merchant at Springfield, and kept a large country store, embracing dry goods, groceries, hardware, books, medicines, bedclothes, mattresses, in fact every thing that the country needed. Lincoln came into the store with his saddle-bags on his arm. He said he wanted to buy the furniture for a single bed. The mattress, blankets, sheets, coverlid, and pillow, according to the figures made by me, would cost seventeen dollars. He said that was perhaps cheap enough; but, small as the sum was, he was unable to pay it. But if I would credit him till Christmas, and his experiment as a lawyer was a success, he would pay then, saying, in the saddest tone, "If I fail in this, I do not know that I can ever pay you." As I looked up at him I thought then, and think now, that I never saw a sadder face.

I said to him, "You seem to be so much pained at contracting so small a debt, I think I can suggest a plan by which you can avoid the debt and at the same time attain your end. I have a large room with a double bed up-stairs, which you are very welcome to share with me." "Where is your room?" said he. "Up-stairs," said I, pointing to a pair of winding stairs which led from the store to my room.

He took his saddle-bags on his arm, went up stairs, set them down on the floor, and came down with the most changed countenance. Beaming with pleasure he exclaimed, "Well, Speed, I am moved!" Mr. Lincoln was then twenty-seven years old—a lawyer without a client, no money, all his earthly wealth consisting of the clothes he wore and the contents of his saddle-bags. . . .

. . . As a lawyer, after his first year, he was acknowledged among the best in the State. His analytical powers were marvelous. He always resolved every question into its primary elements, and gave up every point on his own side that did not seem to be invulnerable. One would think, to hear him present his case in the court, he was giving his case away. He would concede point after point to his adversary until it would seem his case was conceded entirely away. But he always reserved a point upon which he claimed a decision in his favor, and his concession magnified the strength of his claim. He rarely failed in gaining his cases in court.

Mr. Lincoln was a social man, though he did not seek company; it sought him. After he made his home with me, on every winter's night at my store, by a big wood fire, no matter how inclement the weather, eight or ten choice spirits assembled, without distinction of party. It was a sort of social club without organization. They came there because they were sure to find Lincoln. His habit was to engage in conversation upon any and all subjects except politics. . . .

Lincoln had the tenderest heart for any one in distress, whether man, beast, or bird. Many of the gentle and touching sympathies of his nature, which flowered so frequently and beautifully in the humble citizen at home, fruited in the sunlight of the world when he had power and place. He carried from his home on the prairies to Washington the same gentleness of disposition and kindness of heart. Six gentlemen, I being one, Lincoln, [Edward D.] Baker, [John J.] Hardin, and others were riding along a country road. We were strung along the road two and two together. We were passing through a thicket of wild plum and crab-apple trees. A violent wind-storm had just occurred. Lincoln and Hardin were behind. There were two young birds by the roadside too young to fly. They had been blown from the nest by the storm. The old bird was fluttering about and wailing as a mother ever does for her babes. Lincoln stopped, hitched his horse, caught the birds, hunted the nest and placed them in it. The rest of us rode on to a creek, and while our horses were drinking Hardin rode up. "Where is Lincoln?" said one. "Oh, when I saw him last he had two little birds in his hand hunting for their nest." In perhaps an hour he came. They laughed at him. He said with much emphasis, "Gentlemen, you may laugh, but I could not have slept well to-night, if I had not saved those birds. Their cries would have rung in my ears." This is one of the flowers of his prairie life. Now for the fruit.

The last time I saw him was about two weeks before his assassination. He sent me word by my brother James, then in his Cabinet, that he desired to see me before I went home. I went into his office about eleven o'clock. He looked jaded and weary. I staid in the room until his hour for callers was over; he ordered the door closed, and, looking over to where I was sitting, asked me draw up my chair. But instead of being alone, as he supposed, in the opposite direction from where I sat, and across the fire-place from him, sat two humble-looking women. Seeing them there seemed to provoke him, and he said, "Well, ladies, what can I do for you?" One was an old woman, the other young. They both commenced talking at once. The President soon comprehended them. "I suppose," said he, "that your son and your husband are in prison for resisting the draft in Western Pennsylvania. Where is your petition?" The old lady replied, "Mr. Lincoln, I've got no petition; I went to a lawyer to get one drawn, and I had not the money to pay him and come here too; so I thought I would just come and ask you to let me have my boy." "And it's your husband you want?" said he, turning to the young woman. "Yes," said she.

He rung his bell and called his servant, and bade him to go and tell Gen. Dana to bring him the list of prisoners for resisting the draft in Western Pennsylvania.

The General soon came, bringing a package of papers. The President opened it, and, counting the names, said, "General, there are twenty-seven of these men. Is there any difference in degree of guilt?" "No," said the General, "It is a bad case, and a merciful finding." "Well," said the President, looking out of the window and seemingly talking to himself, "these poor fellows have, I think, suffered enough; they have been in prison fifteen months. I have been thinking so for some time, and have so said to Stanton, and he always threatened to resign if they are released. But he has said so about other matters, and never did. So now, while I have the paper in my hand, I will turn out the flock." So he wrote, "Let the prisoners named in the within paper be discharged," and signed it. The General made his bow and left. Then, turning to the ladies, he said, "Now ladies, you can go. Your son, madam, and your husband, madam, is free."

The young woman ran across to him and began to kneel. He took her by the elbow and said, impatiently, "Get up, get up; none of this." But the old woman walked to him, wiping with her apron the tears that were coursing down her cheeks. She gave him her hand, and looking into his face said, "Good-bye, Mr. Lincoln, we will never meet again till we meet in Heaven." A change came over his sad and weary face. He clasped her hand in both of his, and followed her to the door, saying as he went, "With all that I have to cross me here, I am afraid that I will never get there; but your wish that you will meet me there has fully paid for all I have done for you."

We were alone then. He drew his chair to the fire and said, "Speed, I am a little alarmed about myself; just feel my hand." It was cold and clammy.

He pulled off his boots, and, putting his feet to the fire, the heat made them steam. I said overwork was producing nervousness. "No," said he, "I am not tired." I said, "Such a scene as I have just witnessed is enough to make you nervous." "How much you are mistaken," said he; "I have made two people happy to-day; I have given a mother her son, and a wife her husband. That young woman is a counterfeit, but the old woman is a true mother."

This is the fruit of the flower we saw bloom in the incident of the birds.

"He Had a Perfect Eye for Truth"

ISAAC N. ARNOLD

(1815–1885)

POLITICAL ALLY

A pre-war member of the House of Representatives who served as both a Democrat and a Free Soiler, Arnold was sent back to Congress as a Republican in 1860, in the same election that made Lincoln president. Lincoln respected his Chicago ally, and the two remained close during the White House years. After the assassination, Arnold converted his longtime relationship with the President into a biography, *History of Abraham Lincoln and the Overthrow of Slavery,* published in 1866. In it he argued, without much evidence, that Lincoln had harbored abolitionist feelings throughout his life, something of an exaggeration. But otherwise it was a superior work.

Arnold delved deeper into his personal knowledge of Lincoln in an 1869 pamphlet, *Sketch of the Life of Abraham Lincoln,* from which the following recollection is excerpted. Some of the material may strike modern readers as repetitive and fawning, but the recollections were based on years of friendship, and the admiration was clearly genuine and deeply felt. ✣

IS MEMORY WAS CAPACIOUS, READY, AND TENACIOUS. HIS READING WAS LIMITED IN EXTENT, BUT HIS MEMORY WAS SO READY, AND SO RETENTIVE, THAT IN HISTORY, POETRY, AND general literature, no one ever remarked any deficiency. As an illustration of the power of his memory, I recollect to have once called at the White House, late in his Presidency, and introducing to him a Swede and a Norwegian, he immediately repeated a poem of eight or ten verses, describing Scandinavian scenery and old Norse legends. In reply to the expression of their delight, he said that he had read and admired the poem several years before, and it had entirely gone from him, but seeing them recalled it.

The two books which he read most were the Bible and Shakespeare. With these he was very familiar, reading and studying them habitually and constantly. He had great fondness for poetry, and eloquence, and his taste and judgment in each was exquisite. Shakespeare was his favorite poet; Burns stood next. I know of a speech of his at a Burns festival, in which he spoke at length of Burns's poems; illustrating what he said by many quotations, showing perfect familiarity with and full appreciation of the peasant poet of Scotland. He was extremely fond of ballads, and of simple, sad, and plaintive music.

He was a most admirable reader. He read and repeated passages from the Bible and Shakespeare with great simplicity but remarkable expression and effect. Often when going to and from the army, on steamers and in his carriage, he took a copy of Shakespeare with him, and not unfrequently read, aloud to his associates. After conversing upon public affairs, he would take up his Shakespeare, and addressing his companions, remark, "What do you say now to a scene from Macbeth, or Hamlet, or Julius Caesar," and then he would read aloud, scene after scene, never seeming to tire of the enjoyment.

On the last Sunday of his life, as he was coming up the Potomac from his visit to City Point and Richmond, he read aloud many extracts from Shakespeare. Among others, he read, with an accent and feeling which no one who heard him will ever forget, extracts from Macbeth, and among others the following:

> Duncan is in his grave;
> After life's fitful fever, he sleeps well.
> Treason has done his worst; nor steel, nor poison,
> Malice domestic, foreign levy, nothing
> Can touch him farther.

After "treason" had "*done his worst,*" the friends who heard him on that occasion remembered that he read that passage very slowly over twice and with an absorbed and peculiar manner. Did he feel a mysterious presentiment of his approaching fate?

His conversation was original, suggestive, instructive, and playful; and by its genial humor, fascinating and attractive beyond comparison. Mirthfulness and sadness were strongly combined in him. His mirth was exuberant, it sparkled in jest, story, and anecdote; and the next moment those peculiarly sad, pathetic, melancholy eyes, showed a man "familiar with sorrow, and acquainted with grief." I have listened for hours at his table, and elsewhere, when he has been surrounded by statesmen, military leaders, and other distinguished men of the nation, and I but repeat the universally concurring verdict of all, in stating that as a conversationalist he had no equal. One might meet in company with him the most distinguished men, of various pursuits and professions, but after listening for two or three hours, on separating, it was what Lincoln had said that would be remembered. His were the ideas and illustrations that would not be forgotten. Men often called upon him for the pleasure of listening to him. I have heard the reply to an invitation to attend the theater, "No, I am going up to the White House. I would rather hear Lincoln talk for half an hour, than attend the best theater in the world."

"Mr. Lincoln Was Deficient"

MARY OWENS
(1808–1877)
LADY FRIEND

Wealthy and well-read—but also corpulent and far from handsome, as Lincoln later described her—Mary Owens met the future president in the village of New Salem in 1833. On a return visit in 1836, Lincoln began formally courting her, and the following year he proposed. Writing to her from the state capital on 13 December 1836, he declared with what sounds like genuine longing: "Really I have not [been] pleased since I left you." But by the following May, apparently eager now to break off the engagement, he was bluntly warning Mary against marriage: "My opinion is that you had better not do it," he cautioned. "You have not been accustomed to hardship, and it may be more severe than you now imagine." Not surprisingly, Mary released Lincoln from his obligation.

Nevertheless Lincoln was stung by the rejection. He wrote an uncharacteristically cruel letter about the affair in April 1838, admitting that "from her want of teeth [and] weather-beaten appearance in general . . . a kind of notion . . . ran in my head that *nothing* could have commenced at the size of infancy, and reached her present bulk in less than thirtyfive or forty years; and, in short, I was not at all pleased with her." But he also admitted he had been "mortified" when she turned him down. "My vanity was deeply wounded," he confessed, when she "actually rejected me with all my fancied greatness."

Years later, when Lincoln's former law partner, William H. Herndon, set about gathering recollections from Lincoln's contemporaries for a planned biography, he heard about the Owens affair and wrote to her asking for details. Mary Owens Vineyard—she had long since married—complied, and in the end, decisively had the last word. ✣

I THINK I DID ON ONE OCCASION SAY TO MY SISTER, WHO WAS VERY ANXIOUS FOR US TO BE MARRIED, THAT I THOUGHT MR. LINCOLN WAS DEFICIENT IN THOSE LITTLE LINKS WHICH MAKE up the great chain of womans happiness, at least it was so in my case;

not that I believed it proceeded from a lack of goodness of heart, but his training had been different from mine, hence there was not that congeniality which would have otherwise existed. From his own showing you perceive that his heart and hand were at my disposal, and I suppose my feelings were not sufficiently enlisted to have the matter consummated. About the beginning of the year thirty eight, I left Illinois, at which time our acquaintance and correspondence ceased, without ever again being renewed. My father, who resided in Green Co. K[entuck]y, was a gentleman of considerable means, and I am persuaded that few persons placed a higher estimation on education than he did.

We never had any hard feelings towards each other that I knew of. On one occasion did I say to Mr. L—— that I did not believe he would make a kind husband, because he did not tender his services to Mrs. [Bowling] Green [a New Salem neighbor—ed.] in helping of her carry her babe. . . . I thought him lacking in smaller attentions. One circumstance presents itself jut now to my mind's eye. There was a company of us going to Uncle Billy Green's, Mr. L was riding with me, and we had a very bad branch to cross; the other gentlemen were very officious in seeing that their partners got over safely; we were behind, he riding in [front] never looking back to see how I got along; when I rode up beside him, I remarked, you are a nice fellow; I suppose you did not care whether my neck was broken or not. He laughingly replied, (I suppose by way of compliment) that he knew I was plenty smart to take care of myself. In many things he was sensitive almost to a fault. He told me of an incident; that he was crossing a prairie one day, and saw before him a hog mired down, to use his own language; he was rather fixed up and he resolved that he would pass on without looking towards the shoat, after he had gone by, he said, the feeling was irresistible and he had to look back, and the poor thing seemed to say so wistfully—*There now! My last hope is gone,* that he deliberately got down and relieved it from its difficulty.

In many things we were congenial spirits. In politics we saw eye to eye, though since then we have differed as widely as the South is from the North. But me thinks I hear you say, save me from a *political woman! So say I.* The last message I ever received from him was about a year after we parted in Illinois. Mrs. [Elizabeth] Abel visited Ky. and he said to her in Springfield, Tell your Sister, that I think she was a great fool, because she did not stay here and marry me.

Characteristic of the man.

"Somewhat Startled by His Appearance"

CARL SCHURZ

(1829–1906)

GERMAN-AMERICAN REFORMER

Most famous for his later efforts on behalf of civil service reform as secretary of the interior under Rutherford B. Hayes, the German-born Schurz was a disappointed young revolutionary when he emigrated to America in 1849. Here he became an important leader of German-speaking Republicans. Hearing Lincoln debate Stephen A. Douglas in Quincy, Illinois, during the Senate campaign of 1858, Schurz became an instant supporter and lifelong admirer.

As President, Lincoln named Schurz U.S. minister to Spain. Later, realizing Schurz's importance to pro-Union German Americans—a sizable voter bloc represented by as many as one hundred thousand military volunteers—Lincoln named him a brigadier general, then a major general of volunteers. Schurz's war record was not stellar, but his support for the Administration proved important. In later years, Schurz became a U.S. senator from Missouri and an influential newspaper editor in St. Louis and New York.

In this excerpt from his posthumously published *Reminiscences,*

Schurz recalls his first meeting with Lincoln, on a railroad train headed for Quincy the night before the great debate. ✢

———⊶•⊷———

ALL AT ONCE, AFTER THE TRAIN HAD LEFT A WAY STATION, I OB-SERVED A GREAT COMMOTION AMONG MY FELLOW-PASSENGERS, MANY OF WHOM JUMPED FROM THEIR SEATS AND PRESSED eagerly around a tall man who had just entered the car. They addressed him in the most familiar style: "Hello, Abe! How are you?" and so on. And he responded in the same manner: "Good-evening, Ben! How are you, Joe! Glad to see you, Dick!" and there was much laughter at some the things he said, which, in the confusion of voices, I could not understand. "Why," exclaimed my companion [a member of the Republican State Committee—ed.], "there's Lincoln himself!" He pressed through the crowd and introduced me to Abraham Lincoln, whom I then saw for the first time.

I must confess that I was somewhat startled by his appearance. There he stood, overtopping by several inches all those surrounding him. Although measuring something over six feet myself, I had, standing quite near to him, to throw my head backward in order to look into his eyes. That swarthy face with its strong features, its deep furrows, and its benignant, melancholy eyes, is now familiar to every American by numberless pictures. It may be said that the whole civilized world knows and loves it. At that time it was clean-shaven and looked even more haggard and careworn than later when it was framed in whiskers.

On his head he wore a somewhat battered "stove-pipe" hat. His neck emerged, long and sinewy, from a white collar turned down over a thin black necktie. His lank, ungainly body was clad in a rusty black dress coat with sleeves that should have been longer; but his arms appeared so long that the sleeves of a "store" coat could hardly be expected to cover them all the way down to the wrists. His black trousers, too, permitted a very full view of his large feet. On his left arm he carried a gray woolen shawl, which evidently served him for an overcoat in chilly weather. His left hand held a cotton umbrella of the bulging kind, and also a black satchel that bore the marks of long and hard usage. His right he had kept free for hand-shaking, of which there was no end until everybody in the car seemed to be satisfied. I had seen, in Washington and in the West, several public men of rough appearance; but none whose looks seemed quite so uncouth, not to say grotesque, as Lincoln's.

He received me with an off-hand cordiality, like an old acquaintance, having been informed of what I was doing in the campaign [giving anti-slavery speeches, in both English and German, throughout central Illinois—ed.], and we sat down together. In a somewhat high-pitched but pleasant voice he began to talk to me, telling me much about the points he and Douglas had made in the debates at different places, and about those he intended to make at Quincy on the morrow.

When, in a tone of perfect ingenuousness, he asked me—a young beginner in politics—what I thought about this and that, I should have felt myself very much honored by his confidence, had he permitted me to regard him as a great man. But he talked in so simple and familiar a strain, and his manner and homely phrase were so absolutely free from any semblance of self-consciousness or pretension to superiority, that I soon felt as I had known him all my life and we had long been close friends. He interspersed our conversation with all sorts of quaint stories, each of which had a witty point applicable to the subject in hand, and not seldom concluding an argument in such a manner that nothing more was to be said. He seemed to enjoy his own jests in a childlike way, for his unusually sad-looking eyes would kindle with a merry twinkle, and he himself led in the laughter; and his laugh was so genuine, hearty, and contagious that nobody could fail to join in it.

When we arrived at Quincy, we found a large number of friends waiting for him, and there was much hand-shaking and many familiar salutations again. Then they got him into a carriage, much against his wish, for he said that he would prefer to "foot it to Browning's," an old friend's house [former Congressman Orville Hickman Browning, ed.], where he was to have supper and a quiet night. But the night was by no means quiet outside. The blare of brass bands and the shouts of enthusiastic, and not in all cases quite sober, Democrats and Republicans, cheering and hurrahing for their respective champions, did not cease until the small hours.

3. MEMORIES FROM FELLOW LAWYERS

There are two schools of thought when it comes to remembering Lincoln the attorney, and they have coexisted, disparity notwithstanding, for nearly 140 years. The first theory holds that Lincoln was a small-town country lawyer, indifferent about his practice, lax about fees, sloppy about research, but likely to summon cracker-barrel humor and homespun eloquence to sway juries. One New York newspaper dismissed him as an "awkward, common place, hum-drum lawyer . . . of a small country city." The second, more recent school holds that quite the contrary, Lincoln was a successful attorney with a thriving corporate practice, ruthlessly accepting clients whose cases should have repelled him (once representing a slaveowner seeking to reclaim a runaway). This Lincoln was both highly respected and highly paid.

The truth lies somewhere in the middle.

Lincoln was no hack, but he was enough of a hick to be shunned humiliatingly by better-trained colleagues when he was sent out of state once to join a legal team on a major case. (His worst critic there later became one of his cabinet ministers!) And while Lincoln did develop a thriving practice as a sophisticated appeals lawyer, he also found it necessary to travel throughout his central Illinois judicial circuit for months each year in search of business. On the circuit he was part of what amounted to a legal road show, attracting clients whenever he and his fellow lawyers came to a new town to set up court.

If Lincoln was a major lawyer, why did he find it necessary to commit to such a grueling schedule of tedious casework, and for such minuscule compensation, living in dreadful inns, often sleeping two or more lawyers per bed? One psychobiographer recently argued that Lincoln stayed on the road to avoid going home to his contentious wife. But Lincoln so loved his sons it is difficult to believe he would have endured so many prolonged separations if he did not need to do so. The likely explanation is that Lincoln traveled not only in search of income but of political support: often a contender for office, Lincoln cemented bonds during his circuit-riding days that would reap later political dividends.

His fellow lawyers and law clerks agreed, as memories recounted in this section demonstrate, on several key points: whether working in his hometown office or on the road, Lincoln was a witty colleague, a spellbinding courtroom orator, and a more serious student of the law than many early historians acknowledged. Success in the law came, in Lincoln's own words, only through "work, work, work." Lincoln was a hardworking lawyer. ✣

"He Had No Regard for Trivial Things"

HENRY CLAY WHITNEY

(1831–1905)

Fellow Attorney

Whitney practiced law in Urbana, Illinois, but rode the eighth judicial circuit with Lincoln from about 1854 until at least 1858. Years later, after sustaining a serious injury in a hail of gunfire in a Chicago courtroom, Whitney decided to become a Lincoln biographer. He produced a rambling book in 1892, which is nonetheless valuable for its many unique firsthand impressions of Lincoln's day-to-day activities as a circuit-riding lawyer.

Recent scholarship has suggested that Whitney, though a loyal political supporter, may have harbored some resentment for his more famous friend, which he repressed in writing for the public. Nothing he published ever betrayed such a grudge, but Whitney was quite frank in his unforgettable portrait of Lincoln's odd detachment in those unglamorous days. The following reminiscences are excerpted from his 1892 book.

WHEN I FIRST KNEW HIM HIS ATTIRE AND PHYSICAL HABITS WERE ON A PLANE WITH THOSE OF AN ORDINARY FARMER: HIS HAT WAS INNOCENT OF A NAP; HIS BOOTS HAD NO acquaintance with blacking; his clothes had not been introduced to the whisk broom; his carpet-bag was well worn and dilapidated; his umbrella was substantial, but of a faded green, well worn, the knob gone, and the name "A. Lincoln" cut out of white muslin, and sewed in the inside—and for an outer garment a short circular blue cloak, which he got in Washington in 1849, and kept for ten years. He commenced to dress better in the Spring of 1858, and when he was absent from home on political tours usually did so: after he became President he had a servant who kept him considerably "slicked up," but he frequently had to reason Lincoln into fashionable attire, by telling him his appearance was "official."

He probably had as little taste about dress and attire as anybody that ever was born: he simply wore clothes because it was needful and customary; whether they fitted or looked well was entirely above, or beneath, his comprehension.

The judicial circuit, in which Lincoln lived, had, anterior to 1853, consisted of fourteen counties, but in that year had been reduced to eight, viz.: Sangamon, Logan, Tazewell, Woodford, McLean, Dewitt, Champaign, and Vermillion.

Lincoln was the only lawyer who traveled over the entire circuit; he, however, made it a practice to attend every Court, and to remain till the end. This lasted till 1858, when the circuit was radically changed, and Lincoln's attention became much engrossed with politics, which weaned him from a close application to law.

It is to me an interesting reflection, that probably one-half of my readers are not of sufficient age to recollect the time when Mr. Lincoln lived or died.

It also seems interesting to me now to reflect that before he was known to fame, I used to traverse periodically the wild Illinois prairies with this greatest of men—these prairies now teeming with a dense and busy life, then quite as desolate and almost as solitary as at Creation's dawn—that our means of travel were limited to home-made vehicles, that we were accustomed to put up at homely farm-houses and village inns; and sleep two in a bed, and eight in a room; that our business was transacted, and our daily bread earned, in unkempt court-rooms where ten months in the year the town boys played at marbles or rudimentary circus; that our offices were ambulatory, being located now on the sunny side of a Court House, then under the shade of a friendly tree, and, anon, on the edge of a sidewalk.

It is strange to contemplate that in those comparatively recent but primitive days, Mr. Lincoln's whole attention should have been engrossed in petty controversies or acrimonious disputes between neighbors about trifles; that he should have puzzled his great mind in attempting to decipher who was the owner of a litter of pigs, or which party was to blame for the loss of a flock of sheep, by foot rot; or whether some irascible spirit was justified in avowing that his enemy had committed perjury; yet I have known him to give as earnest attention to such matters as later he gave to affairs of State. . . .

The semi-annual shopping of the country districts was transacted during Court week; the wits and county statesmen contributed their stock of pleasantry and philosophy; the local belles came in to see and be seen; and the Court House from "early dawn till dewy eve," and the tavern from dewy eve to early morn, were replete with bustle, business, energy, hilarity, novelty, irony, sarcasm, excitement and eloquence. At the tavern the lawyers slept two in a bed and three or four beds were located in one room: at meals, the Judge, lawyers, suitors, jurors, witnesses, Court officers, and prisoners out on bail all ate together and carried on in a running conversation all along the line of a long dining room.

When one Court was through, the Judge and lawyers would tumble into a farmer's wagon, or a carryall, or a succession of buggies, and trundle off across the prairie to another court, stopping by the way at a farm house for a chance dinner.

In this kind of unsteady, nomadic life, Lincoln passed about four months each year; he had no clerk, no stenographer, no library, no method or system of business, but carried his papers in his hat or coat pocket. The consideration and trial of each case began and ended with itself; he was continually roused to devise a new policy—new tactics—fresh expedients, with each new retainer. . . .

As for Lincoln, he had three different moods, if I may so express myself: first, a *business* mood, when he gave strict and close attention to business, and banished all idea of hilarity, i.e., in counseling or in trying cases, there was no trace of the joker; second, his *melancholy* moods, when his whole nature was immersed in Cimmerian [*sic*] darkness; third, his *don't-care-whether-school-keeps-or-not* mood, when no irresponsible "small boy" could be so apparently careless, or reckless of consequences.

To illustrate the "style" of business in court by something very common: the first term of [Judge David W.] Davis' Court I attended, the Judge was calling through the docket for the first time, in order to dispose of such cases as could be done summarily, and likewise to sort the chaff from the wheat, when he came across a long bill in chancery, drawn by an excellent, but somewhat indolent lawyer, on glancing at which he exclaimed, "Why, brother Snap, how *did* you rake up energy enough to get such a long bill?" "Dunno, Judge," replied the party addressed, squirming in his seat and uneasily scratching his head. The Judge unfolded and held up the bill: "Astonishing, ain't it? Brother Snap did it. Wonderful, eh! Lincoln?" This amounted to an order on Lincoln to heave a joke in at this point, and he was ready, of course; he had to be, he never failed. "It's like the lazy preacher," drawled he, "that used to write long sermons, and the explanation was, he got to writin', and was too lazy to stop." This was doubtless improvised and forgotten at once, as I never heard of his repeating it. It was rather feeble, but it was better than the stock word, "Humph!" so often printed as a reply, but never really uttered, and it is literally true that

> he could not ope
> His mouth, but out there flew a trope.

He *always* had a reply, and it was *always* pertinent, and frequently irresistibly funny, but the pity is that his funniest stories don't circulate in polite society or get embalmed in type. . . .

Mr. Lincoln had no method, system or order in his exterior affairs; he had no library, no clerk, no stenographer; he had no commonplace book, no index *rerum,* no diary. Even when he was President and wanted to preserve a memorandum of anything, he noted it down on a card and stuck it in a drawer or in his vest pocket. But in his mental processes and operations, he had the most complete system and order. While outside of his mind all was anarchy and confusion, inside all was symmetry and method. His mind was his workshop; he needed no office, no pen, ink and paper; he could perform his chief labor by self-introspection.

Nor was Lincoln, of necessity, physically alone when in a state of complete mental seclusion. I have frequently seen him, in the midst of a Court session, with his mind completely withdrawn from the busy scene before his eyes, as completely abstracted as if he was in absolute and unbroken solitude.

I can recollect of two distinct occasions when he saw me plainly, and shook hands with me rather mechanically, yet with apparent intelligence, and notwithstanding this, he repeated the same performance, but with zeal and enthusiasm, within one hour thereafter, assuring me that I was mistaken, that he had not spoken to me before, that day. These solitary habits, the jocular and grotesque side of his character: his intense and inordinate caution and secretiveness, as well as his desire to avoid all display, constitute sufficient and ample reasons why it was so difficult for ordinary persons who expect great results to be ostentatiously done, to understand and realize that Lincoln was a marvelously great man—a character as great as his deeds, and having a logical position in politics and statesmanship.

In his social life, characteristics, tastes and habits, he was the most simple, guileless, and unsophisticated man that it was possible to be. At the table, he ate what came first, without discrimination or choice; whatever room at the hotel came handy or whatever bed he came to first he took without criticism or inspection; if the fire needed replenishing and no one was at hand, he made no inquiry or complaint, but hunted up an axe, took off his coat, and went vigorously at work at the wood pile. In a law suit, even with others, he would either make the chief argument, or examine the witnesses, or search out authorities, draft the pleadings, affidavits, or motions, and even, if necessary, run . . . errands in connection with the case. If any lawyer, old or young, wanted assistance or advice, he was always ready and patient to accord it; no one, however humbler, felt any constraint in his presence at any time; nor did anyone, despite his clownish antics, feel any inclination or possess any warrant, to become unduly familiar or take liberties with him. . . .

He had no regard for trivial things, or for mere forms, manners, politeness, etiquette, official formalities, fine clothes, routine, or red tape; he disdained a bill-of-fare at table; a programme at theatre; or a license to get married. The pleadings in a law suit, the formal compliments on a social introduction, the exordium of peroration of a speech, he either wholly ignored or cut as short as he could.

State dinners—levees—and the magniloquent and hypocritical forms of diplomacy, were "gall and wormwood" to him.

He did not favor or countenance slander or other suits in tort; he condemned all irrelevant questions in a legal examination; he was terribly impatient if any lawyer, in arguing a case, "beat about the bush" or talked "wide of the mark," or at random in the case; he had little patience with litigation, except such as grew naturally out of business affairs, or the necessary exigencies of social life. In all his political campaigns, the flags and bunting were nothing to him; he was thinking, rather, of the statistics, how many votes were probable, and what the tendencies of political thought were, to change opinions and votes.

"A Splendid and Imposing Figure"

WILLIAM H. HERNDON
(1818–1891)
LAW PARTNER

Lincoln's last law partner and one of his most important biographers, Herndon devoted the years after the assassination to laborious research, gathering personal reminiscences from his old friend's earliest acquaintances. When it came to firsthand observations of Lincoln, however, Herndon was perhaps the most valuable witness of all. He shared a Springfield law office with his senior (but equal) partner from 1844 until Lincoln departed for Washington to take the oath of office as president in 1861. Their partnership was never formally dissolved; on paper, at least, it survived until Lincoln's death in 1865.

Herndon was also one of Lincoln's most ardent admirers. More liberal on the slavery question, he later claimed to have moved Lincoln politically, but probably exaggerated his influence. Herndon experienced no end of difficulty gathering together Lincoln's biography. His book, subtitled *The True Story of a Great Life,* did not appear until 1889, by which time its author was fighting a losing battle against alcoholism and poverty. Although some scholars have dismissed the effort as sensationalist, and fatally clouded by his hatred for Mary Lincoln, the book does contain incontestably valuable passages—like the following recollections of Lincoln the talented attorney and indulgent father. ✢

A LAW OFFICE IS A DULL, DRY PLACE SO FAR AS PLEASURABLE OR INTERESTING INCIDENTS ARE CONCERNED. IF ONE IS IN SEARCH OF STORIES OF FRAUD, DECEIT, CRUELTY, BROKEN promises, blasted homes, there is no better place to learn them than a law office. But to the majority of persons these painful recitals are anything but attractive, and it is well perhaps that it should be so. In the office, as in the court room, Lincoln, when discussing any point, was never arbitrary or insinuating. He was deferential, cool, patient, and respectful. When he reached the office, about nine o'clock in the morning, the first thing he did was to pick up a newspaper, spread himself out on an old sofa, one leg on a chair, and read aloud, much to my discomfort. Singularly enough Lincoln never read any other way but aloud. This habit used to annoy me almost beyond the point of endurance. I once asked him why he did so. This was his explanation: "When I read aloud two senses catch the idea: first, I see what I read; second, I hear it, and therefore I can remember it better." He never studied law books unless a case was on hand for consideration—never followed up the decisions of the supreme courts, as other lawyers did. It seemed as if he depended for his effectiveness in managing a law suit entirely on the stimulus and inspiration of the final hour. He paid but little attention to the fees and money matters of the firm—usually leaving all such to me. He never entered an item in the account book. If any one paid money to him which belonged to the firm, on arriving at the office he divided it with me. If I was not there, he would wrap up my share in a piece of paper and place it in my drawer—marking it with a pencil, "Case of Roe *vs.* Doe.—Herndon's half. . . .

. . . He exercised no government of any kind over his household. His children did much as they pleased. Many of their antics he approved, and he restrained them in nothing. He never reproved them or gave them a fatherly frown. He was the most indulgent parent I have ever known. He was in the habit, when at home on Sunday, of bringing his two boys, Willie and Thomas—or "Tad"—down to the office to remain while his wife attended church. He seldom accompanied her there. The boys were absolutely unrestrained in their amusement. If they pulled down all the books from the shelves, bent the points of all the pens, overturned inkstands, scattered law-papers over the floor, or threw the pencils in the spittoon, it never disturbed the serenity of their father's good-nature. . . . Had they s——t in Lincoln's hat and rubbed it on his boots, he would have laughed and thought it smart. . . . Frequently absorbed in thought, he never observed their mischievous but destructive pranks—as his unfortunate partner did, who thought much, but said nothing—and, even if brought to his attention, he virtually encouraged their repetition by declining to show any substantial evidence of parental disapproval. . . .

Mr. Lincoln never had a confidant, and therefore never unbosomed himself to others. He never spoke of his trials to me or, so far as I knew, to any of his friends. It was a great burden to carry, but he bore it sadly enough and without a murmur. I could always realize when he was in distress, without being told. He was not exactly an early riser, that is, he never usually appeared in the office till about nine o'clock in the morning. I usually preceded him an hour. Sometimes, however, he would come down as early as seven o'clock—in fact, on one occasion I remember he came down before daylight. If, on arriving at the office, I found him in, I knew instantly that a breeze had sprung up over the domestic sea, and that the waters were troubled. He would either be lying on the lounge looking skyward, or doubled up in a chair with his feet resting on the sill of a back window. He would not look up on my entering, and only answered my "Good morning" with a grunt. I at once busied myself with pen and paper, or ran through the leaves of some books; but the evidence of his melancholy and distress was so plain, and his silence so significant, that I would grow restless myself, and finding some excuse to go to the court-house or elsewhere, would leave the room.

The door of his office opening into a narrow hallway was half glass, with a curtain on it working on brass rings strung on wire. As I passed out on these occasions I would draw the curtain across the glass, and before I reached the bottom of the stairs I could hear the key turn in the lock, and Lincoln was alone in his gloom.

One phase of Lincoln's character, almost lost sight of in the commonly accepted belief in his humility and kindly feeling under all circumstances, was his righteous indignation when aroused. In such cases he was the most fearless man I ever knew. I remember a murder case in which we appeared for the defense, and during the trial of which the judge—a man of ability far inferior to Lincoln's—kept ruling against us. Finally, a very material question, in fact one around which the entire case seemed to revolve, came up, and again the Court ruled adversely. The prosecution was jubilant, and Lincoln, seeing defeat certain unless he recovered his ground, grew very despondent. The notion crept into his head that the Court's rulings, which were absurd and almost spiteful, were aimed at him, and this angered him beyond reason. He told me of his feelings at dinner, and said: "I have determined to crowd the Court to the wall and regain my position before night." From that time forward it was interesting to watch him. At the reassembling of court he arose to read a few authorities in support of his position. In his comments he kept within the bounds of propriety just far enough to avoid a reprimand for contempt of court.

He characterized the continued rulings against him as not only unjust but foolish; and, figuratively speaking, he pealed the Court from head to foot. I shall never forget the scene. Lincoln had the crowd, a portion of the bar, and the jury with him. He knew that fact, and it, together with the belief that injustice had been done him, nerved him to a feeling of desperation. He was wrought up to the point of madness. When a man of large heart and head is wrought up and mad, as the old adage runs, "he's mad all over." Lincoln had studied up the points involved, but knowing full well the calibre of the judge, relied mostly on the moral effect of his personal bearing and influence. He was alternately furious and eloquent, pursuing the Court with broad facts and pointed inquiries in marked and rapid succession. I remember he made use of this homely incident in illustration of some point: "In early days a party of men went out hunting for a wild boar. But the game came upon them unawares, and scampering away they all climbed the trees save one, who, seizing the animal by the ears, undertook to hold him, but despairing of success cried out to his companions in the trees, 'For God's sake, boys, come down and help me let go.'" The prosecution endeavored to break him down or even "head him off," but all to no purpose. His masterly arraignment of law and facts had so effectually badgered the judge that, strange as it may seem, he pretended to see the error in his former position, and finally reversed his decision in Lincoln's favor.

"He Was Too Serious for Comfort"

JOHN H. LITTLEFIELD

(B. 1835)
LAW STUDENT

Littlefield, the son of a Cicero, Illinois, carriage-maker, studied law in the Lincoln-Herndon office in Springfield from 1859 to 1860 and enjoyed many opportunities to observe Lincoln as he grew in national stature en route to the presidential nomination. During the Civil War, Lincoln named him to a post in the Treasury Department, but then Littlefield made a radical career change. He left the law to return to his first love, art, and Lincoln eventually became his most famous subject. He produced a famous Lincoln deathbed scene in 1865, and also a handsome portrait that inspired a best-selling 1869 engraving published by Pate & Co., of New York. Charles Sumner told Littlefield: "Our martyred President lives in this engraving."

Littlefield published his personal recollections of Lincoln in *The Independent* in 1895. The following excerpt is drawn from that article. ✣

MR. LINCOLN USED TO COME TO THE OFFICE AT ODD TIMES, HAVING NO PARTICULAR HOURS. HE DID A GOOD DEAL OF WORK AT HOME. HE WAS A VERY INDUSTRIOUS MAN. Whenever he had anything of interest on hand he was a hard worker. One of the secrets of his success was his ability to "bone down" to hard work. Whenever he had an important case on hand he would withdraw himself more or less from society, and would devote himself with great care to the case. At such times he would display wonderful power of concentration. He used to go about in a sort of brown study. Sometimes he would take his young son Tad and, throwing him over his shoulder, would go out on the prairie. The boy being on his shoulder would seemingly give him the necessary ballast so that he could, in nautical parlance, go to windward well. By the time he returned to the house he would have a clear conception of the case and have the knotty points unravelled.

While in the office considering some important case, I have frequently known him to put the book down, and all at once break out: "Do you know what this case makes me think of?" and then he would tell a story. In this way humor would enliven jurisprudence.

One day he came to the office and had scarcely opened the door when he exclaimed: "John, did I ever tell you that rat story?" Then he told, with great earnestness, about a man who stammered, and who tried to cure himself of the habit by whistling.

He was very democratic and approachable. Frequently in going along the street he would meet some old friend and start in: "By the way, I am just reminded of a story," and he would stop in the street and tell the yarn. There was no postponement on account of the weather.

It must not be understood, however, that Mr. Lincoln was not a very serious man; in fact, he was one of the most serious men I have ever known. You might say that his seriousness was a species of melancholy. He was much of the time a sad, serious man, and a good deal of his humor was evidently for the purpose of counteracting these moods and throwing you off your guard; because when he got into these moods he was too serious for comfort.

But it was surprising to see what a fund of anecdotes he had. No story could be told but he could match it, and "go one better." He had a remarkable memory. He remembered faces well, and could, on the instant, recall where he had seen people and how he had made their acquaintance.

All his life he was an extreme temperance man. At one time he belonged to the "Sons of Temperance" in Springfield, and in his early manhood frequently made temperance speeches. In his habits he was a strict temperance man.

And he was a remarkably clean man in his conversation. He endured some *risqué* stories on account of their wit. Once a young man came to the office, and he undertook to tell a broad story that had no wit in it. He told it simply because it was broad. Lincoln took him by the nape of his neck and ordered him out of the office, saying: "Young man, never come here with such a story. If there had been any real wit in it you might have been pardoned."

Lincoln did not seem to have any pleasures common to men of the world. He was not a great eater nor a drinker. The nearest approach I ever knew him to make toward entertainment or pleasure was after he was nominated at Chicago. He used to play barn ball there nearly every day—throwing a ball up against a brick building and trying to catch it. I often used to play with him. That is the nearest approach to pleasure I ever saw him make [in fact, Lincoln did not go to Chicago for the 1860 convention, although he was known to play ball in Springfield—ed.].

In literature he seemed to prefer Shakespeare and Burns. He could recite whole passages from Shakespeare, notably from "Hamlet," with wonderful effect. He was very fond of the drama. In "Hamlet," he claimed that the passage commencing: "Oh! my offence is rank," etc., was better than the soliloquy. He said that the great beauty of Shakespeare was the power and majesty of the lines, and argued that even an indifferent actor could hold an audience by the power of the text itself.

Lincoln was what you would call an odd, a singular man. A large part of his time was spent in study and thought. He was a very deep and close thinker, and a genuine logician.

In regard to religious matters he did not talk to Herndon on those subjects. Herndon one day intimated to me that he did not know what Lincoln believed. All the talk in Herndon's book about Lincoln's religious belief is clap-trap. Whatever he may have believed in early days, he did not talk with Herndon on the subject of religion during the time I was there. He rarely attended church; he spent Sunday at home, quietly. Mrs. Lincoln attended the Presbyterian church, and the children were brought up in that faith.

This is what Mr. Lincoln said to me on the subject of religion, the nearest approach he ever made to talking on the subject: One day he stopped his work and said to me, suddenly, "John, it depends a great deal on how you state a case. When Daniel Webster stated a case, it was half argument. Now," said he, "you take the subject of predestination; you state it one way, and you cannot make much of it; you state it another, and it seems quite reasonable."

Lincoln always manifested interest in everybody with whom he associated. When you first met him and studied him he impressed you with being a very sad man and a very kind man. He struck you as being a man who would go out of his way to serve you. There was about him a sense of self-abnegation. Lincoln impressed me as a man who had arrived at a point in Christianity without going to church that others struggle to attain, but do not reach, by going. I never in all my life associated with a man who seemed so ready to serve another. He was a very modest man in his demeanor, and yet gave you an impression of strong individuality. In his freedom of intercourse with people he would seem to put himself on par with everybody; and yet there was within him a sort of reserved power, a quiet dignity which prevented people from presuming on him, notwithstanding he had thrown down the social bars. A person of less individuality would have been trifled with.

In money matters he was economical and thrifty, because he did not seem to have much desire to spend money on himself. He did not smoke, chew or drink; and a suit of clothes would last him a long time because he was not restless in his manner.

In regard to his attire I used to wonder why he did not appear to be "dressed up"; for when I looked at him a second time I would see that he was as well dressed as the average lawyer, wearing a plain broadcloth suit, a high hat, and fine boots. But his angularity and individuality were so pronounced that the clothes seemed to lose their character, as it were.

Lincoln displayed great eagerness to learn on all subjects from everybody. When he was introduced to persons his general method was to entertain them by telling them a story, or else cross-question them along the line of their work, and soon draw from them about all the information they had.

As a lawyer, in his opening speech before the jury, he would cut all the "dead wood" out of the case. The client would sometimes become alarmed, thinking that Lincoln had given away so much of the case that he would not have anything left. After he had shuffled off the unnecessary surplusage he would get down to "hard pan," and state the case so clearly that it would soon be apparent he had enough left to win the case with. In making such concessions he would so establish his position in fairness and honesty that the lawyer on the opposite side would scarcely have the heart to oppose what he contended for.

He would not undertake a case unless it was a good one. If it was a poor case he would almost invariably advise the client to settle it the best way he could. When a case had been misrepresented to him and he afterward discovered the fact in court, he would throw it up then and there. One of the great secrets of his success was the reputation he had of being a thoroughly honest lawyer. Long before he became President he was known by the *sobriquet* of "Honest Old Abe." He had become such a synonym for honesty that everybody was willing to yield assent to nearly every proposition he advanced, either in or out of court.

"A Very Poor Hater"

LEONARD SWETT
(1825–1889)
LAWYER AND POLITICAL ALLY

No political lieutenant was more loyal to Lincoln than Swett, and few were as useful. The Maine-born Illinois lawyer met Lincoln in 1849, pledged in 1856 to support him for whatever office he aspired to, and four years later helped secure for him the Republican presidential nomination. Unlike many early supporters, Swett never hounded Lincoln for patronage rewards, or at least did not receive any. He ran unsuccessfully for Congress in Illinois in 1862, losing to an anti-administration Democrat, yet went on to champion Lincoln's renomination at the party convention in 1864. Ten years after Lincoln's death, Swett, then a thriving Chicago lawyer, represented Robert Lincoln in his successful legal action to have his mother committed for insanity. The first excerpt here was printed in Francis B. Carpenter's 1866 volume, *Six Months at the White House;* the second analysis was prepared the same year for Lincoln biographer William H. Herndon. ✤

AS HE ENTERED THE TRIAL, WHERE MOST LAWYERS WOULD OB-JECT HE WOULD SAY HE "RECKONED" I WOULD BE FAIR TO LET THIS IN, OR THAT; AND SOMETIMES, WHEN HIS ADVERSARY could not quite prove what Lincoln knew to be the truth, he "reckoned" it would be fair to admit the truth to be so-and-so. When he did object to the court, and when he heard his objections answered, he would often say, "Well, I reckon I must be wrong." Now, about the time he had practiced this three-fourths through the case, if his adversary didn't understand him, he would wake up in a few minutes learning that he had feared the Greeks too late and find himself beaten. He was wise as a serpent in the trial of a cause, but I have had too many scares from his blows to certify that he was harmless as a dove. When the whole thing was unraveled, the adversary would begin to see that what he was so blandly giving away was simply what he couldn't get and keep. By giving away six points and carrying the seventh he carried his case, and the whole case hanging on the seventh, he traded away everything which would give him the least aid in carrying that. Any man who took Lincoln for a simple-minded man would very soon wake up with his back in a ditch.

He had very great kindness of heart. His mind was full of tender sensibilities; he was extremely humane, yet while these attributes were fully developed in his character and unless intercepted by his judgment controlled him, they never did control him contrary to his judgment. He would strain a point to be kind, but he never strained to breaking. Most of men of such kindly feeling are controlled by this sentiment against their judgment, or rather that sentiment beclouds their judgment. It was never so with him. He would be just as kind and generous as his judgment would let him be—no more. . . .

He was certainly a very poor hater. He never judged men by his like or dislike for them. If any given act was to be performed, he could understand that his enemy could do it just as well as anyone. If a man had maligned him, or been guilty of personal ill-treatment and abuse, and was the fittest man fir the place, he would put him in his Cabinet just as soon as he would his friend. I do not think he ever removed a man because he was his enemy, or because he disliked him.

The great secret of his power as an orator, in my judgment, lay in the clearness and perspicuity of his statements. When Lincoln had started a case, it was always more than half argued and the point more than half won. The first impression he generally conveyed was that he had stated the case of his adversary better and more forcibly than his opponent could state it himself. He then answered that state of facts fairly and fully, never passing by, or skipping over a bad point. When this was done, he presented his own case. There was a feeling when he argued a case, in the mind of any man who listened to him, that nothing had been passed over; yet if he could not answer the objections he argued in his own mind and himself arrived at the conclusion to which he was leading others; he had very little power of argumentation. The force of his logic was in conveying to the minds of others the same clear and thorough analysis he had in his own, and if his own mind failed to be satisfied, he had no power to satisfy anybody else. His mode and force of argument was in stating how he had reasoned upon the subject and how he had come to his conclusion, rather than original reasoning to the hearer, and as the mind of [the] listener followed in the groove of his mind, his conclusions were adopted. He never made sophistical [*sic*] argument in his life, and never could make one. I think he was of less real aid in trying a thoroughly bad cause than any man I was ever associated with. If he could not grasp the whole case and master it, he was never inclined to touch it.

From the commencement of his life to the close, I have sometimes doubted whether he ever asked anybody's advice about anything. He would listen to everybody; he would hear everybody, but he never asked for opinions. I never knew him in trying a law-suit to ask the advice of any lawyer he was associated with. As a politician and as a President he arrived at all his conclusions from his own reflections, and when his opinion was once formed he never had any doubt but what it was right.

4. MEMORIES FROM JOURNALISTS AND HUMORISTS

There were no White House news conferences in Lincoln's day. Presidents issued no press releases, hired no press secretaries, and seldom spoke for attribution to reporters. During the Civil War, the word "interview" meant a private meeting, not a journalistic interrogation.

On the other hand, the culture of the era encouraged relationships between journalists and politicians that would today be regarded as conspiratorial. In Lincoln's day, newspapers were rigidly allied with one political party or the other and their correspondents not only covered, but advised candidates. A reporter named Horace White, who was assigned to the 1858 Lincoln-Douglas debates for the pro-Republican *Chicago Press & Tribune,* for example, became so vital a part of that campaign that he wrote Lincoln after he lost: "I don't think it possible for you to feel more disappointed than I do."

As President, the beleaguered Lincoln became a bit more aloof from the press. Asked once to provide an advance copy of a speech to the press, Lincoln refused, denouncing the practice as "a source of endless mischief." Nonetheless, Lincoln's private secretary, John G. Nicolay, was a former journalist, and had Lincoln lived he probably would have replaced him with yet another friendly reporter, Noah Brooks.

Among Lincoln's favorite newspapermen were humorists. The President's way with a funny story was renowned enough in his own time to inspire books like *Old Abe's Jokester* and *Humors of Uncle Abe,* but Lincoln protested that he was merely a "retailer" of jokes he had read and memorized. Among his favorite humorists were Charles F. Browne (who wrote under the pseudonym "Artemus Ward"), Robert Henry Newell (who published under the name "Orpheus C. Kerr," a play on the words "office-seeker"), and David R. Locke ("Petroleum V. Nasby" to his readers), who met and admired the President. When a dour cabinet minister protested once after Lincoln read aloud from an Artemus Ward collection, the President explained sadly: "With all the fearful strain that is upon me night and day, if I did not laugh I should die."

Ward's and Nasby's stories were full of tongue-twisting drolleries related in thick country accents, difficult to parse today, but screamingly funny to Lincoln. It is fair to say that they became his favorite "journalists."

This section presents several firsthand observations by professional newspaper writers—serious as well as comic. The former are generally laudatory, since opposition, pro-Democratic reporters were granted no opportunity to study Lincoln in detail. Memories from journalists are thus unavoidably rosy, although publisher Horace Greeley, whose memories are included here, sparred with Lincoln on policy issues throughout the war. ✣

"No Man Living Has a Kinder Heart"

NOAH BROOKS

(1830–1903)

JOURNALIST

Brooks served during the last two and a half years of the war as Washington correspondent of the *Sacramento Daily Union,* an assignment that frequently brought him to the White House to cover Abraham Lincoln.

The President granted him broad access, partly because he was fond of the reporter, and partly because Brooks's articles, dispatched west by pony express, took so long to appear in print that they seldom posed a threat to the secrecy of administration policy. Brooks signed all his articles with the pen name "Castine," a name he derived from the Maine town where he was born.

Like the President, a onetime Whig who had converted to the Republicans, Brooks's journalism was pro-Union, pro-emancipation, and pro-Lincoln. Lincoln was probably planning to reward him in 1865 by naming him White House private secretary, but he was assassinated before he could announce a replacement for outgoing secretary John G. Nicolay.

The following recollections begin with Brooks's Washington report of 7 November 1863—a rich portrait of the President performing the kind of constituent services that modern chief executives abandoned long ago. Next are extracts from a piece Brooks wrote for *Harper's New Monthly Magazine* soon after Lincoln's assassination and then excerpts from the full-length biography he published in 1888. ✢

WHEN THE PRESIDENT LIVES IN TOWN HE COMMENCES HIS DAY'S WORK LONG BEFORE THE CITY IS ASTIR, AND BEFORE BREAKFAST HE CONSUMES TWO HOURS OR MORE IN WRITING, reading, or studying some of the host of subjects which he has on hand. It may be the Missouri question, the Maryland imbroglio, the Rosecrans removal question [issues of border state loyalty and the future of a Union general—ed.], or the best way to manage some great conflicting interest which engrosses his attention, but these two best hours of the fresh day are thus given to the work. Breakfast over, by nine o'clock he has directed that the gate which lets in the people shall be opened upon him, and then the multitude of cards, notes, and messages which are in the hands of his usher come in upon him. Of course, there can be no precedence, except so far as the President makes it, and as a majority of the names sent in are new to him, it is very much of a lottery as to who will get in first. The name being given to the usher by the President, that functionary shows in the gratified applicant, who may have been cooling his heels outside for five minutes or five days but is now ushered into a large square room furnished with green stuff, hung around with maps and plans, a bad portrait of Jackson over the chimney piece, a writing table piled up with documents and papers, and two large, draperied windows looking out upon the broad Potomac and commanding the Virginia heights opposite on which numberless military camps are whitening in the sun.

The President sits at his table and kindly greets whoever comes. To the stranger he addresses his expectant, "Well?" and to the familiar acquaintances he says, "And how are you today, Mr. ——?" though it must be confessed that he likes to call those whom he likes by their first names, and it is "Andy" (Curtin) [governor of Pennsylvania—ed.], "Dick" (Yates) [governor of Illinois—ed.], and so on. [William H.] Seward [the secretary of state—ed.] he always calls "Governor," and [Montgomery] Blair and [Edward] Bates [postmaster general and attorney general, respectively—ed.] is "Judge." The rest are plain "Mister," never "Secretary." With admirable patience and kindness, Lincoln hears his applicant's requests and at once says what he will do, though he usually asks several questions, generally losing more time than most businessmen will by trying to understand completely each case, however unimportant, that comes before him. He is not good at dispatching business but lets every person use more time than he might if the interview were strictly limited to the real necessities of the case. Consequently, Lincoln cannot see a tithe of the people who daily besiege his antechamber. In his anxiety to do equal and exact justice to all, he excludes or delays those who might see him sooner if he did not try to do so much. No man living has a kinder heart than Abraham Lincoln, and all who meet him go away thoroughly impressed with the preponderance of those two lovable and noble traits of his character.

Is the petitioner a poor widow who wants a writership in one of the departments? The President has read her credentials and asked a question or two in his quiet but shrewd way. He takes a card on which he writes a plain request to a cabinet minister to give the bearer what she craves, and the grateful woman goes out, blessing the good-natured President whose very next act may be to receive a distinguished foreign diplomat whose government is hovering on the doubtful verge of an American war; or it may be a Brigadier wanting promotion, an inventor after a contract, a curiosity hunter with an autograph book, a Major General seeking a command, a lady with a petition for a pass to Richmond, a cabinet minister after a commission for a favorite, a deputation asking an impossibility, or a committee demanding an impertinence; it may be all or any of these who come next, and the even-tempered statesman who patiently sits there, interlarding the dull details of business with a good-natured joke or anecdote, must wisely and quickly decide upon questions which vary in importance from a small favor to a humble dependent to the adjustment of one of the momentous national interests of the times.

No man but Mr. Lincoln ever knew how great was the load of care which he bore, nor the amount of mental labor which he daily accomplished. With the usual perplexities of the office—greatly increased by the unusual multiplication of places in his gift—he carried the burdens of the civil war, which he always called "This great trouble." Though the intellectual man had greatly grown meantime, few persons would recognize the hearty, blithesome, genial, and wiry Abraham Lincoln of earlier days in the sixteenth President of the

United States, with his stooping figure, dull eyes, care-worn face, and languid frame. The old, clear laugh never came back; the even temper was sometimes disturbed; and his natural charity for all was often turned into an unwonted suspicion of the motives of men, whose selfishness cost him so much wear of mind. Once he said, "Sitting here, where all the avenues to public patronage seem to come together in a knot, it does seem to me that our people are fast approaching the point where it can be said that seven-eighths of them were trying to find how to live at the expense of the other eighth."

It was this incessant demand upon his time, by men who sought place or endeavored to shape this policy, that broke down his courage and his temper, as well as exhausted his strength. Speaking of the "great flood-gates" which his doors daily opened upon him, he said, "I suppose I ought not to blame the aggregate, for each abstract man or woman thinks his or her case a peculiar one, and must be attended to, though all others be left out; but I can see this thing growing every day." And at another time, speaking of the exhaustive demands upon him, which left him in no condition for more important duties, he said, "I sometimes fancy that every one of the numerous grist ground through here daily, from a Senator seeking a war with France down to a poor woman after a place in the Treasury Department, darted at me with thumb and finger, picked out their especial piece of my vitality, and carried it off. When I get through with such a day's work there is one word which can express my condition, and that is—*flabbiness.*" There are some public men who can now remember, with self-reproaches, having increased with long evening debates that reducing "flabbiness" of the much-enduring President. . . .

It is generally agreed that Mr. Lincoln's slowness was a prominent trait of his character; but it is too early, perhaps, to say how much of our safety and success we owe to his slowness. It may be said, however, that he is today admired and beloved as much for what he did not do as for what he did. He was well aware of the popular opinion concerning his slowness, but was only sorry that such a quality of mind should sometimes be coupled with weakness and vacillation. Such accusation he thought to be unjust. Acknowledging that he was slow in arriving at conclusions, he said that he could not help that; but he believed that when he did arrive at conclusions they were clear and "stuck by." He was a profound believer in his own fixity of purpose, and took pride in saying that his long deliberations made it possible for him to stand by his own acts when they were once resolved upon.

No man was ever more free from affectation, and the distaste that he felt for form, ceremony, and personal parade was genuine. Yet he was not without a certain dignity of bearing and character that commanded respect. At times, too, he rebuked those who presumed too far on his habitual good-nature and affable kindness. . . .

An old acquaintance of the President, whom he had not seen for many years, visited Washington. Lincoln desired to give him a place. Thus encouraged, the visitor, who was an honest man, but wholly inexperienced in public affairs or in business, asked for a high office. The

President was aghast, and said: "Good gracious! Why didn't he ask to be Secretary of the Treasury and have done with it?" Afterward, he said: "Well, now, I never thought M. had anything more than average ability, when we were young men together—and he wants to be superintendent of the mint!" He paused, and added, with a queer smile: "But, then, I suppose he thought the same thing about me, and—here I am."

"He Showed Remarkable Tact"

—◆•••◆—

HENRY VILLARD

(1835–1900)

JOURNALIST

After the election of 1860, the *New York Herald* sent the German-born Villard to Springfield to report on the activities of President-Elect Lincoln. It was a remarkable achievement for a young journalist who, two years earlier, had been reporting on politics for German-language newspapers. The correspondent met Lincoln during the 1858 Senate campaign, finding him "most approachable, good natured, and full of wit and humor." He encountered him again in 1859, and easily won access to Lincoln, reporting on his campaign for the White House.

Villard's dispatches were collected for a slim 1941 volume, but these were news and feature reports of Lincoln's day-to-day activities as he prepared to assume office. A fuller assessment of the man he knew can be found in Villard's memoirs. Both sources are used for the following recollection of Lincoln on the eve of the presidency and civil war.

Villard went on to a hugely successful career as a railroad tycoon. ✤

HIS OLD FRIENDS, WHO HAVE BEEN USED TO A GREAT INDIF-
FERENCE AS TO THE "OUTER MAN" ON HIS PART, SAY THAT "ABE
IS PUTTING ON AIRS." BY THIS THEY REFER TO THE FACT THAT
HE is now wearing a brand new hat and suit and that he has com-
menced cultivating the—with him—unusual adornment of whiskers.

But, these late outward embellishments to the contrary notwithstanding, a Broadway tailor would probably feel no more tempted to
consider Lincoln as coming up to his artistic requirements of a model
man than Peter Cooper. The angularity of the Presidential form, and
its habitual *laissez aller,* preclude a like possibility. We venture to say
that Fifth Avenue snobs, if unaware who he was, would be horrified at
walking across the street with him. And yet, there is something about
the man that makes one at once forget these exterior shortcomings
and feel attracted toward him.

The President-elect being the very embodiment of good humor, it
seems as though from this fact, much that happens about him partakes
of a comical character. Some days ago, a tall Missourian marched into
the reception room. Seeing the tall form of the President rise before
him, and not knowing what to say, he ejaculated "I reckon one is about
as big as the other." "Let us measure" was the instantaneous reply; and
the Missourian was actually placed against the wall, told "to be honest,
and stand flat on his heels," and his height measured with a stick.

Mr. Lincoln's personal appearance is the subject of daily remark
among those who have known him formerly. Always cadaverous, his

aspect is now almost ghostly. His position is wearing him terribly. Letters threatening his life are daily received from the South, occasionally, also, a note of warning from some Southerner who does not like his principles, but would regret violence. But these trouble him little compared with the apprehended difficulty of conciliating the South without destroying the integrity of his own party. The present aspect of the country, I think, augurs one of the most difficult terms which any President has yet been called to weather; and I doubt Mr. Lincoln's capacity for the task of bringing light and peace out of the chaos that will surround him. A man of good heart and good intention, he is not firm. The times demand a Jackson.

It was a most interesting study to watch the manner of his intercourse with his callers. As a rule, he showed remarkable tact in dealing with each of them, whether they were rough-looking Sangamon County farmers still addressing him familiarly as "Abe," sleek and pert commercial travelers, staid merchants, sharp politicians, or preachers, lawyers, or other professional men. He showed a very quick and shrewd perception of and adaptation to individual characteristics and peculiarities. He never evaded a proper question, or failed to give a fit answer. He was ever ready for an argument, which always had an original flavor, and, as a rule, he got the better in the discussion. There was, however, one limitation to the freedom of his talks with his visitors. A great many of them naturally tried to draw him out as to his future policy as President regarding the secession movement in the

South, but he would not commit himself. The most remarkable and attractive feature of those daily "levees," however, was his constant indulgence of his story-telling propensity. Of course, all the visitors had heard of it and were eager for the privilege of listening to a practical illustration of his pre-eminence in that line. He knew this, and took special delight in meeting their wishes. He never was at a loss for a story or an anecdote to explain a meaning or enforce a point, the aptness of which was always perfect. His supply was apparently inexhaustible, and the stories sounded so real that it was hard to determine whether he repeated what he had heard from others, or had invented [them] himself.

None of his hearers enjoyed the wit—and wit was an unfailing ingredient—of his stories half as much as he did himself. It was a joy indeed to see the effect upon him. A high-pitched laughter lighted up his otherwise melancholy countenance with thorough merriment. His body shook all over with gleeful emotion, and when he felt particularly good over his performance, he followed his habit of drawing up his knees, with his arms around them, up to his very face, as I had seen him do in 1858. I am sorry to state that he often allowed himself altogether too much license in the concoction of the stories. He seemed to be bent upon making his hit by fair means or foul.

In other words, he never hesitated to tell a coarse or even outright nasty story, if it served his purpose. All his personal friends could bear testimony on this point. It was a notorious fact that this fondness for low talk clung to him even in the White House. More than once I heard him "with malice aforethought" get off purposely some repulsive fiction in order to rid himself of an uncomfortable caller. Again and again I felt disgust and humiliation that such a person should have been called upon to direct the destinies of a great nation in the direst period of its history. Yet his achievements during the next few years proved him to be one of the great leaders of mankind in adversity, to whom low leanings only set off more strikingly his better qualities. At the time of which I speak, I could not have persuaded myself that the man might possibly possess true greatness of mind and nobility of heart. I do not wish to convey the idea, however, that he was mainly given to trivialities and vulgarities in his conversation; for, in spite of his frequent outbursts of low humor, his was really a very sober and serious nature, and even inclined to gloominess to such an extent that all his biographers have attributed a strongly melancholic disposition to him.

"He Said Wonderfully Witty Things"

DAVID R. LOCKE ("PETROLEUM VESUVIUS NASBY")

(1833–1888)

HUMORIST

Locke was serving as the editor of a Findlay, Ohio, newspaper when in 1861 he encountered a neighborhood drunk circulating a petition calling for the deportation of all the local African-Americans. Outraged, Locke penned a satiric letter supporting the purge and published it over the signature of a ridiculous bigot for whom he invented the pseudonym "Petroleum V. Nasby." The article was well received, and Locke began writing additional Nasby letters. A collection entitled *The Nasby Papers* appeared in 1864. By this time he was a particular favorite of President Lincoln, who found the absurd posturing of Locke's stock pro-Confederate character wildly funny, no doubt aware that the satires made the Southern, white-supremacist causes seem laughable.

Locke met Lincoln on several occasions, later writing warmly—and seriously—about their encounters. The recollection that follows comes from a piece he published in the compendium *Reminiscences of Lincoln by Distinguished men of his Time,* published the year of Locke's death, 1888. It is followed by a different sort of recollection—an imaginary encounter between the Civil War President and his fictional critic, "Petroleum V. Nasby," with its intentional misspellings and quaint dialects fully intact. ✤

——◆◆◆——

I SUCCEEDED IN OBTAINING AN INTERVIEW WITH HIM AFTER THE CROWD HAD DEPARTED, AND I ESTEEM IT SOMETHING TO BE PROUD OF THAT HE SEEMED TO TAKE A LIKING TO ME. HE TALKED to me without reserve. It was many years ago, but I shall never forget it.

He sat in the room with his boots off, to relieve his very large feet from the pain occasioned by continuous standing; or, to put it in his own words: "I like to give my feet a chance to breathe." He had removed his coat and vest, dropped one suspender from his shoulder, taken off his necktie and collar, and thus comfortably attired, or rather unattired, he sat tilted back in one chair with his feet upon another in perfect ease. He seemed to dislike clothing, and in privacy wore as little of it as he could. I remember the picture as though I saw it but yesterday.

Those who accuse Lincoln of frivolity never knew him. I never saw a more thoughtful face, I never saw a more dignified face, I never saw so sad a face. He had humor of which he was totally unconscious, but it was not frivolity. He said wonderfully witty things, but never from a desire to be witty. His wit was entirely illustrative. He used it because, and only because, at times he could say more in this way, and better illustrate the idea with which he was pregnant. He never cared how he made a point so that he made it, and he never told a story for the mere sake of telling a story. When he did it, it was for the purpose of illustrating and making clear a point. He was essentially epigrammatic and parabolic. He was a master of satire, which was at times as blunt as a meat-ax, and at others as keen as a razor; but it was always kindly except when some horrible injustice was its inspiration, and then it was terrible. Weakness he was never ferocious with, but intentional wickedness he never spared.

In this interview the name came up of a recently deceased politician of Illinois, whose undeniable merit was blemished by an overweening vanity. His funeral was very largely attended: "If General —— had known how big a funeral he would have had," said Mr. Lincoln, "he would have died years ago."

But with all the humor in his nature, which was more than humor because it was humor with a purpose (that constituting the difference between humor and wit), his was the saddest face I ever looked upon.

His flow of humor was a sparkling spring gushing out of a rock —the flashing water had a somber background which made it all the brighter. Whenever merriment came over that wonderful countenance it was like a gleam of sunshine upon a cloud—it illuminated, but did not dissipate. The premonition of fate was on him then; the shadow of the tragic closing of the great destiny in the beyond had already enveloped him.

At the time, he said he should carry the State on the popular vote, but that Douglas would, nevertheless, be elected to the Senate, owing to the skillful manner in which the State had been districted in his interest. "You can't overturn a pyramid, but you can undermine it; that's what I have been trying to do."

He undermined the pyramid that the astute Douglas had erected, most effectually. It toppled and fell very shortly afterward. . . .

I met Lincoln again in 1859, in Columbus, Ohio, where he made a speech, which was only a continuation of the Illinois debates of the year before. Douglas had been previously brought there by the Democracy, and Lincoln's speech was, in the main, an answer to Douglas. It is curious to note in this speech that Lincoln denied being in favor of negro suffrage, and took pains to go out of his way to affirm his support of the law of Illinois forbidding the intermarriage of whites and negroes.

I asked him if such a denial was worth while, to which he replied:

"The law means nothing. I shall never marry a negress, but I have no objection to any one else doing so. If a white man wants to marry a negro woman, let him do it—*if the negro woman can stand it.*"

By this time his vision had penetrated the future, and he had got a glimmering of what was to come. In his soul he knew what he should have advocated, but he doubted if the people were ready for the great movement of a few years later. Hence his halting at all the half-way houses.

"Slavery," said he, "is doomed, and that within a few years. Even Judge Douglas admits it to be an evil, and an evil can't stand discussion. In discussing it we have taught a great many thousands of people to hate it who had never given it a thought before. What kills the skunk is the publicity it gives itself. What a skunk wants to do is to keep snug under the barn — in the day-time, when men are around with shot-guns."

The discussions with Douglas made him the Republican nominee for the Presidency, and elected him President.

The "Nasby Letters," which I began in 1861, attracted his attention, and he was very much pleased with them. He read them regularly. He kept a pamphlet which contained the first numbers of the series in a drawer in his table, and it was his wont to read them on all occasions to his visitors, no matter who they might be, or what their business was. He seriously offended many of the great men of the Republican Party in this way. Grave and reverent Senators who came charged to the brim with important business — business on which the fate of the nation depended — took it ill that the President should postpone the consideration thereof while he read them a letter from "Saint's Rest, wich is in the state uv Noo Jersey," especially as grave statesmen, as a rule, do not understand humor, or comprehend its meaning or effect.

Lincoln also seized eagerly upon everything that Orpheus C. Kerr wrote, and he knew it all by heart.

It was in 1863 that I received a letter from Lincoln, which illustrates two points in his character; viz., his reckless generosity, and the caution which followed close at its heels.

This is the conclusion of the letter:

"Why don't you come to Washington and see me? Is there no

place you want? Come on and I will give you any place you ask for—*that you are capable of filling—and fit to fill.*"

What led to this was, he had read a letter of mine which pleased him, and the generosity of his nature prompted him to write me to come and see him, and that was supplemented by an offer to give me *any place I asked for.* After he had finished the letter and added his signature, it occurred to him that to promise a man of whom he knew but little, except through the medium of the press, *any place that he might ask for,* was rather risky. So he added a dash, and likewise the saving clause, "*that you are capable of filling,*" and, to guard himself entirely, "*that you are fit to fill.*"

I did go and see him, but not to ask for a place. He gave me an hour of his time, and a delightful hour it was. The end of the terrible struggle was within sight, the country he loved so well had passed through the throes of internecine strife and demonstrated its right to live, and the great and good man was on the eve of passing from labor to reward. It was a fact that treason was more rampant at the North than ever; that great dangers were still threatening; but the army was actually an army, and the loyal sentiment of the North had shown that it could be depended upon. He bubbled over with good feeling; he expressed a liking for my little work, which I have not the assurance to put upon paper, and I departed. [A comic version of such a meeting by "Nasby" follows—ed.]

• • •

I felt it my dooty to visit Washinton. The misarable condishon the Dimocrisy find themselves into sinse the elecshun, makes it nessary that suthin be did, and therefore I determind to see wat cood be effectid by a persnel intevew with the Presdent.

Interdoosin myself, I opened upon him delikitly, thus:

"Linkin," sez I, "ez a Dimocrat, a free-born Dimocrat, who is prepared to die with neetnis and dispatch, and on short notis, fer the inalienable rite uv free speech—knoin also that you er a goriller, a feendish ape, a thirster after blud, I speek."

"Speek on," says he.

"I am a Ohio Dimocrat," sez I, "who has repoodiatid Valandigum."

"Before or sinse the elecshun did yoo repoodiate him?" sez he.

"Sinse," retorted I.

"I thot so," sed he. "I would hev dun it too, hed I bin you," continuered he, wish a goriller-like grin.

"We air now in favor uv a wiggeorus prosecushen uv the war, and we want you to so alter yoor polisy that we kin act with you, corjelly," sez I.

"Say on," sez he.

"I will. We don't want yoo to change yoor polisy, materially. We air modrit. Anxshus to support yoo, we ask yoo to adopt the follerin' trifling changis:

"Restoar to us our habis corpusses, as good ez new.

"Arrest no moar men, wimmin and children, fer opinyun's saik.

"Repele the ojus confisticashen bill, wich irrytaits the Suthern mind and fires the Suthern hart.

"Do away with drafts and conskripshens.

"Revoak the Emansipashen proclamashen, and give bonds that you'll never ishoo a nother.

"Do away with tresury noats and sich, and pay nuthin but gold.

"Protect our dawters frum nigger eqwality.

"Disarm yoor nigger soljers, and send back the niggers to their owners to conciliate them.

"Offer to assoom the war indetednis uv the South, and plej the Government to remoonerate our Suthrin brethrin fer the losses they hev sustaned in this onnatral war.

"Call a convenshen uv Suthern men and sech gileless Northern men ez F. Peerce, J. Bookanon, Fernandough Wood and myself, to agree upon the terms of reunion."

"Is that all?" sez the goriller.

"No," sez I, promptly. "Ez a garantee uv good faith to us, we shel insist that the best haff uv the orifises be given to Dimocrats who re-poodiate Valandigum. Do this, Linkin, and yoo throw lard ile on the trubbled waters. Do this and yoo rally to yoor support thowsends uv noble Dimocrats who went out uv offis with Bookanon, and hev bin gittin ther whisky on tick ever sinse. We hev maid sakrifises. We hev repoodiated Valandigum—we care not ef he rots in Canady—we are willin to jine the war party, reservin to ourselvs the poor privilidg uv dictatin how and on what prinsipples it shel be carried on. Linkin! Goriller! Ape! I hev dun."

The President replide that he wood give the matter serious considerashen. He wood menshen the idee uv resinin to Seward, Chais and Blair, and wood address a serculer to the Postmasters et settry, an see how menny uv em wood be willin' to resine to accommodait Dimocrats. He hed no doubt sevral wood do it to wunst.

"Is ther any littel thing I kin do fer yoo?"

"Nothin pertikler. I wood eccept a small Post orifis, if sitooatid within ezy range uv a distilry. My politikle daze is well-nigh over. Let me see the old party wunst moar in the assendency—let these old eyes onct moar behold the Constooshn ez it is, the Union ez it wuz, and the Nigger ware he ought a be, and I will rap the mantel uv privit life arownd me, and go inz delirum tremens happy. I hev no ambishen. I am in the sear and yaller leef. These whitnin lox, them sunken cheak, warn me that age and whisky hev dun ther perfeck work, and that I shell soon go hents. Linkin, scorn not my wurds, I hev sed. Adoo."

So sayin I wavd my hand impressively and walked away.

PETROLEUM V. NASBY,
Paster uv sed Church, in charge.

"Their Deliverer from Bondage"

SYLVANUS CADWALLADER

(CA. 1825–)

WAR CORRESPONDENT

For three years, Cadwallader covered Ulysses S. Grant for the *Chicago Times,* becoming one of the ablest of the war correspondents. In the view of a New York rival: "He was not diverted in his search by fatigue, danger, or any other obstacle."

The journalist was at the front when President Lincoln visited Grant's headquarters toward the end of the war. Cadwallader observed him entering camp, to the surprise of a Union sentry who failed to recognize Lincoln, then riding along the front, where he was at once spotted—and greeted warmly—by a group of African-Americans.

Notwithstanding his unique access to the war's most important commander, Cadwallader's reminiscence remained unissued until 1955, when Lincoln scholar Benjamin P. Thomas rescued it from oblivion, edited it, and saw to its publication. ✧

GEN. GRANT'S HEADQUARTERS WERE ESTABLISHED AT CITY POINT ON THE EVENING OF JUNE 15TH AND A FEW TENTS PITCHED FOR THE OFFICERS. MY OWN TENT WAS UNDER THE umbrageous branches of a large mulberry tree which afforded protection from the blistering sunshine, until it had to be removed to conform to the general camp arrangement. By night of the 16th all was regularly laid out and adjusted. Headquarters proper were in the form of a parallelogram, with the two ends, and the north side closely filled with tents. The south side was open. The west end extended to the bluff bank of the Appomattox, perhaps fifty to sixty feet in height. . . .

From the 17th to the 20th the James was covered with vessels and transports which had followed the army with supplies, and with them came swarms of civilians—employees of the Sanitary and Christian Commissions—sutlers—pretended volunteer nurses—and greedy sightseers who managed to get there to gratify their morbid curiosity. They swarmed around the wharves, filled up the narrow avenues at the landing between the six-mule teams which stood there by the acre, plunged frantically across the road in front of your horse wherever you rode, plied everybody with ridiculous questions about "the military situation," invaded the privacy of every tent, stood around every mess-table till invited to eat unless driven away, and wandered around at nearly all hours.

They congregated especially in the vicinity of headquarters, standing in rows just outside of the guard-line, staring at Gen. Grant and staff, pointing out the different members of the latter to each other, and seizing upon every unfortunate darky belonging to headquarters who came within their reach, and asking all manner of impertinent questions: "Does Gen. Grant smoke? Where does he sleep and eat? Does he drink? Are you sure he is not a drinking man? Where's his wife? What became of his son that was with him at Vicksburg? Which is Gen. Grant? What? Not that little man?" And so on by the hour. For several days headquarters resembled a menagerie.

On June 21st about one o'clock p.m., a long, gaunt bony looking man with a queer admixture of the comical and the doleful in his countenance that reminded one of a professional undertaker cracking a dry joke, undertook to reach the general's tent by scrambling through a hedge and coming in alone. He was stopped by a hostler and told to "keep out of here." The man in black replied that he thought Gen. Grant would allow him inside. The guard finally called out: "No sanitary folks allowed inside" [a reference to Sanitary Commission volunteers—ed.]. After some parleying the man was obliged to give his name, and said he was Abraham Lincoln, President of the United States, seeking an interview with Gen. Grant! The guard saluted, and allowed him to pass. Grant recognized him as he stepped under the large "fly" in front of his tent, rose and shook hands with him cordially, and then introduced him to such members of the staff as were present and unacquainted.

It transpired that the President had just arrived on the "City of Baltimore," and was accompanied by his son "Tad"; Asst. Sec. of the Navy, [Gustavus Vasa] Fox; Mr. Chadwick, proprietor of the Willard Hotel, as purveyor for the party; and the Marine Band. The conversation took a wide, free-and-easy range until dinner was announced. The President was duly seated, ate much as other mortals, managed to ring in three capital jokes during the meal, and kept everybody on the lookout for others, till the party rose.

He was naturally desirous of riding to the front, so at four o'clock horses were brought up. Mr. Lincoln was mounted on Grant's thorough-bred "Cincinnatus," the general on "Egypt," and "Tad," on Grant's black pacing pony "Jeff Davis." Accompanied by a large proportion of the staff, and a cavalry escort, the party rode to Gen. Wright's headquarters, where Gen. Meade and staff met them. The location commanded as good a view of Petersburg as could then be had from our lines. Maps were examined, the position of the army explained, its future operations discussed, the steeples and spires of the city observed as well as the dust and smoke would allow, national airs were played by the bands, the enemy's works on the opposite side of the Appomattox inspected, and after a stay of an hour and a half the party started on its return to headquarters.

On the way out many persons recognized Mr. Lincoln. The news soon spread, and on the return ride, the road was lined with weather-beaten veterans, anxious to catch a glimpse of "Old Abe." One cavalry private had known him in Illinois. Mr. Lincoln shook him by the hand, as an old familiar acquaintance, to the infinite admiration of all bystanders.

The noticeable feature of the ride was the passing a brigade of negro troops. They were lounging by the roadside, and when he approached came rushing by hundreds screaming, yelling, shouting: "Hurrah for the Liberator; Hurrah for the President," and were wild with excitement and delight. It was a genuine spontaneous outburst of love and affection for the man they looked upon as their deliverer from bondage. The President uncovered as he rode through their ranks, and bowed on every hand to his sable worshipers.

"A Great Persuader"

HORACE GREELEY

(1811–1872)

NEWSPAPER PUBLISHER

Although best remembered for his exhortation, "Go West, young man," Greeley was also the founder and influential editor of the *New York Tribune,* whose support for the Union war effort was considered crucial by the Lincoln Administration. Over the years, however, Lincoln and Greeley often crossed swords. Always a staunch Republican, Greeley had thought seriously in 1858 about supporting Lincoln's opponent for the U.S. Senate, Democrat Stephen A. Douglas. Nor did Greeley favor Lincoln for the presidential nomination of 1860, though he backed him once he became the nominee. Later, he publicly criticized Lincoln for being too slow on emancipation, opposed Lincoln's renomination in 1864, and urged a premature armistice with the Confederacy in 1865.

Greeley later published an autobiography in which he recalled his associations with the wartime President, whom he came late and somewhat grudgingly to admire, as the first excerpt reveals. The reminiscence concludes with an extract from a speech by Greeley made about Lincoln that first found its way into print nearly twenty years after the publisher's death. ✢

THERE ARE THOSE WHO SAY THAT MR. LINCOLN WAS FORTUNATE IN HIS DEATH AS IN HIS LIFE: I JUDGE OTHERWISE. I HOLD HIM MOST INAPT FOR THE LEADERSHIP OF A PEOPLE INVOLVED IN desperate, agonizing war; while I deem few men better fitted to guide a nation's destinies in time of peace. Especially to I deem him eminently fitted to soothe, to heal, and to reunite in bonds of true, fraternal affection a people just lapsing into peace after years of distracting, desolating internal strife. His true career was just opening when an assassin's bullet quenched his light of life.

Mr. Lincoln entered Washington the victim of a grave delusion. A genial, quiet, essentially peaceful man, trained in the ways of the bar and the stump, he fully believed that there would be no civil war—no serious effort to consummate disunion. His faith in reason as a moral force was so implicit that he did not cherish a doubt that his Inaugural Address, whereon he had bestowed much thought and labor, would, when read throughout the South, dissolve the Confederacy as frost is dissipated by the vernal sun. I sat just behind him as he read it, on a bright, warm, still March day, expecting to hear its delivery arrested by the crack of a rifle aimed at his heart; but it pleased God to postpone the deed, though there was forty times the reason for shooting him in 1860 [the inauguration was actually in 1861—ed.] than there was in '65, and at least forty times as many intent on killing or having him killed. No shot was then fired, however; for his hour had not yet come.

Almost everyone has personal anecdotes of "Old Abe." I knew

him more than sixteen years, met him often, talked with him familiarly; yet, while multitudes fancy that he was always overflowing with jocular narrations or reminiscences, I cannot remember that I ever heard him tell an anecdote or story.

Here was an heir of poverty and insignificance, obscure, untaught, buried throughout his childhood in the primitive forests, with no transcendent, dazzling abilities, such as make their way in any country, under any institution, but emphatically in intellect, as in station, one of the millions of strivers for a rude livelihood who, though attaching himself stubbornly to the less popular party, and especially so in the State which he had chosen as his home, did nevertheless become a central figure of the Western Hemisphere, and an object of honor, love, and reverence throughout the civilized world. . . . He was not a born king of men, ruling by the restless might of his natural superiority, but a child of the people, who made himself a great persuader, therefore a leader, by dint of firm resolve, and patient effort, and dogged perseverance. He slowly won his way to eminence and renown by ever doing the work that lay next to him—doing it with all his growing might—doing it as well as he could, and learning by his failure, when failure was encountered, how to do it better. Wendell Phillips [a leading Abolitionist of the day—ed.] once coarsely said: "He grew because we watered him," which was only true insofar as this—he was open to all impressions and influences, and gladly profited by all the teachings of events and circumstances, no matter how adverse or unwelcome. There was probably no year of his life in which he was not a wiser, cooler, better man than he had been the year preceding. . . .

. . . The Republic needed to be passed through chastening, purifying fires of adversity and suffering; so these came and did their work, and the verdure of a new national life springs greenly from their ashes. Other men were helpful to the great renovation, and nobly did their part in it; yet, looking back through the lifting mists of seven eventful, tragic, trying, glorious years, I clearly discern that the one providential leader, the indispensable hero of the great drama—faithfully reflecting even in his hesitations and seeming vacillations the sentiment of the masses—fitted by his very defects and shortcomings for the burden laid upon him, the good to be wrought out through him, was Abraham Lincoln.

5. MEMORIES FROM FOREIGN OBSERVERS

From the time Alexis de Tocqueville toured America and published his acclaimed observations, the New World became an inviting, almost irresistible muse for writers from the Old. Charles Dickens, among others, followed suit. And when the Civil War created two Americas instead of one, the flow of foreign observers seemed to grow exponentially.

Many regarded Abraham Lincoln as a principal tourist destination. Something about the frontier giant, who seemed so ingratiatingly informal, yet so piercingly intelligent, so—how else to say it? —quintessentially American, compelled attention from these travelers. European reporters came, too. Compared to their own monarchs, Lincoln seemed quite approachable. Their dispatches reveal a people's ruler in crisis, lacking the trappings of the Old World, but boasting a native intelligence and wisdom that even the most jaded and dandified foreign correspondent could not overlook.

Lincoln was not always comfortable with foreign visitors. When the Prince of Wales passed through his hometown of Springfield, Illinois, during a celebrated 1860 American tour that was generating more press coverage than that year's presidential election campaign, the Republican candidate declined to go to the depot to meet him, believing it would be undignified. Characteristically, he later told a reporter that he had stayed in his office instead, meeting "so many sovereigns during the day that really the Prince had come and gone" before he knew it. As President, he grew more comfortable with such formalities, welcoming the most ornately costumed ambassadors and emissaries into the White House as part of his official routine.

Lincoln's extraordinary, almost universal appeal to even the most well-born, well-educated foreign visitors remains one of the most fascinating pockets of Civil War–era literature. The "critics" whose views are recalled in the following pages came to the United States believing its president would prove an embarrassment. Instead they found an intellectual revelation—and an American original. ✤

"He Is Simple, Serious, and Full of Good Sense"

ERNEST DUVERGIER DE HAURANNE

(1842–1876)

FRENCH JOURNALIST

A latter-day Tocqueville (who was in fact a friend of his father), Duvergier de Hauranne visited America in 1864 at age twenty-two, armed with a well-worn copy of *Democracy in America* and a determination to fill his own notebooks with firsthand observations.

The French visitor grew into an ardent supporter of the Union war effort and came to admire Lincoln for "that virtue of perseverance and determination which is . . . the American virtue *par excellence.*" He met the President in the closing months of the war.

Returning home, Duvergier de Hauranne published two books advocating reform in France, served with distinction in the Franco-Prussian war, and was elected to the Chamber of Deputies in 1871. His American notes were published as a series of articles, and later in a book entitled *Huit Mois en Amérique,* from which the following excerpt is taken. Duvergier de Hauranne planned a second trip to the United States, but died young, ending a promising career in letters and politics.

A T LAST I HAVE MET THE PRESIDENT. I WAS PRESENTED TO HIM IN HIS OFFICE BY MR. SUMNER AT THE HOUR WHEN, LIKE ST. LOUIS UNDER HIS OAK TREE [A REFERENCE TO KING LOUIS IX of France—ed.], he receives petitions from his people. For a foreigner the White House possesses a certain prestige; and besides, I have been taught discretion by our customs to the point where I wouldn't dare go past its threshold without a guide or without a special invitation from the great personage who lives there. Yet its doors stand open to every American: like a church, it is everybody's house. At all hours of the day, you will find curious or idle people milling about in the great reception room where the President holds his popular audiences. It is said that some visitors—country bumpkins, no doubt—cut pieces from the silk curtains to take home as souvenirs of their pilgrimage. You may think that a policeman or at least a guard has been posted. Not at all! There is only a notice asking visitors to respect the furnishings, which belong to the government.

We went up a flight of stairs, we opened a door, and suddenly we were in the majestic presence of the President. At the far end of the room, his back to the window behind a huge desk piled so high with papers that it seemed to enclose him like the walls of a confessional, "Father Abraham" was seated on a low chair and writing on his knees with his long legs bent double. In front of him stood a woman who had come to ask a favor; dressed in her best attire and standing respectfully before him, she leaned forward and whispered into his ear something that he proceeded to write down on his pad. Mingling pertness with humility, she favored him with her sweetest smiles and most penetrating glances; but the President, a grave and somewhat hurried judge, urged her to come to the point, questioned her briefly and rather brusquely, diligently scribbling at his notes all the while, his attitude clearly indicating by his manner that she was wasting his time and that he was neither stupid nor easygoing enough to be taken in by her wiles.

Five or six other people, soldiers and lower-class women, were silently awaiting their turn, sitting in a row along the wall. The lady in velvet was soon sent away, and the President rose to receive us; it was then that his great height was revealed. I looked up and saw a bony face, framed by a shock of carelessly combed hair, a flat nose and a wide mouth with tightly closed lips. His face was angular and furrowed by deep wrinkles. His eyes were strangely penetrating and held a sardonic expression; he seemed sad and preoccupied, bent under the burden of his immense task. His posture was awkward and like nothing I've ever seen before—partly rigid and partly loose-jointed; he doesn't seem to know how to carry his great height. We all opened our mouths after the customary handshake, I to pay him a compliment, Mr. Sumner to explain who I was, and he himself to respond to my remark and to pretend that he already knew my name. His voice is far from musical; his language is not flowery; he speaks more or less like an ordinary person from the West and slang comes easily to his tongue.

Beyond this, he is simple, serious and full of good sense. He made some comments on Mr. Everett and on the unrealistic hopes the Democratic party entertained four years ago that it could impose its policies on the victorious Republicans. These remarks may have been lacking in sparkle, but the thought behind them was subtle and witty. There was not a single burst of clownish laughter, not a single remark in doubtful taste, not one of the "jokes" for which he is famous. We shook hands again and left him to his chores. I took away from this ten-minute interview an impression of a man who is doubtless not very brilliant, not very polished, but worthy, honest, capable, and hard-working. I think the Europeans who have spoken and written about him have been predisposed to consider it amusing to exaggerate his odd ways—either that or else they went to the White House expecting to see some splendid, decorative figure, wearing a white tie and behaving in a manner both courteous and condescending like some sort of republican monarch. What a stupid and egregious error to expect that Abraham Lincoln, the former Mississippi boatman, could have the manners of a king or a prince!

"He Works Hard and Does Little"

EDWARD DICEY

(1832–1911)

BRITISH JOURNALIST

This perceptive British writer spent half of 1862 covering the American Civil War, filing his incisive reports for both the *Spectator* and *Macmillan's Magazine*.

He then assembled his articles for a book, published the following year, that featured his frank impressions of Abraham Lincoln, some of which are excerpted here. They have permanent value because they were recorded before Lincoln's assassination and deification—when he still seemed, in Dicey's view, undisguisedly flawed.

Dicey went on to a distinguished career in English letters, spending nineteen years as editor of the London Observer and writing books on Egypt and Bulgaria.✥

—•◆•—

A SHREWD, HARD-HEADED, SELF-EDUCATED MAN, WITH SENSE ENOUGH TO PERCEIVE HIS OWN DEFICIENCIES, BUT WITHOUT THE INSTINCTIVE GENIUS WHICH SUPPLIES THE PLACE OF learning, he is influenced by men whom he sees through, but yet cannot detect. "An honest man" may be the "noblest work of God," but he is not the noblest product of humanity, and when you have called the President "honest Abe Lincoln," according to the favorite phrase of the American press, you have said a great deal, doubtless, but you have also said *all* that can be said in his favor. He works hard, and does little; and unites a painful sense of responsibility to a still more painful sense, perhaps, that his work is too great for him to grapple with.

Personally, his aspect is one which, once seen, cannot easily be forgotten. If you take the stock of English caricature of the typical Yankee, you have the likeness of the President. To say that he is ugly, is nothing. [This sentence appeared in Dicey's magazine report, but was deleted from his book—ed.] To say that his figure is grotesque is to convey no adequate impression. Fancy a man six-foot, and thin *out of* proportion, with long bony arms and legs, which, somehow, seem to be always in the way, with large rugged hands, which grasp you like a vise when shaking yours, with a long scraggy neck, and a chest too narrow for the great arms hanging by its side; add to this figure, a head, coconut shaped and somewhat too small for such a stature, covered with a rough, uncombed and uncombable lank dark hair, that stands out in every direction at once; a face furrowed, wrinkled, and indented, as though it had been scarred by vitriol; a high narrow forehead; and, sunk deep beneath bushy eyebrows, two bright, somewhat dreamy eyes, that seemed to gaze through you without looking at you; a few irregular blotches of black bristly hair in the place where beard and whiskers ought to grow; a close-set, thin-lipped, stern mouth, with two rows of large white teeth; and a nose and ears, which have been taken by mistake from a head of twice the size.

Clothe this figure, then, in a long, tight, badly-fitting suit of black, creased, soiled, and puckered up at every salient point of the figure—and every point of this figure is salient—put on large, ill-fitting boots, gloves too long for the long bony fingers, and a fluffy hat, covered to the top with dusty, puffy crepe [probably as a sign of mourning for his late son, Willie—ed.]; and then add to all this an air of strength, physical as well as moral, and a strange look of dignity coupled with all this grotesqueness, and you will have the impression left upon me by Abraham Lincoln. You would never say he was a gentleman: you would still less say he was not one. There are some women about whom no one ever thinks in connection with beauty, one way or the other—and there are men to whom the epithet of "gentlemanlike" or "ungentlemanlike" appears utterly incongruous, and of such the President is one. Still there is about him a complete absence of pretension, and an evident desire to be courteous to everybody, which is the essence, if not the outward form, of high breeding. There is a softness, too, about his smile, and a sparkle of dry humor about his eye which redeem the expression of his face, and remind me more of the late Dr. [Thomas] Arnold [legendary British headmaster—ed.], as a child's recollection recalls him to me, than any other face I can call to memory.

On the occasion when I had the honor of passing some hours in company with the President, the gathering was a very small one, and consisted of persons with all of whom, except myself, he was personally acquainted. I have no doubt, therefore, that he was as much at his ease as usual, and yet the prevailing impression left upon my mind was that he felt uncomfortable. There was a look of depression about his face, which I am told by those who see him daily, was habitual to him, even before the then recent death of his child, whose loss he felt acutely. You cannot look upon his worn, bilious, anxious countenance, and believe it to be that of a happy man. In private life, his disposition, unless re-port and physiognomy both err, is a somber one; but, coupled with this, he has a rich fund of dry, Yankee humor, not inconsistent, as in the case of the nation itself, with a sort of habitual melancholy.

It was strange to me to witness the terms of perfect equality on which he appeared to be with everybody. Occasionally some of his in-terlocutors called him "Mr. President," but the habit was to address him simply as "Sir." There was nothing in his own manner, or in that of his guests, to have shown a stranger that the President of the United States was one of the company. He spoke but little, and seemed to prefer others talking to him to talking himself. But when he did speak, his remarks were always shrewd and sensible. The conversation, like that of all American official men I have ever met with, was unrestrained in the presence of strangers to a degree perfectly astonishing. It is a regard for English, rather than for American, rules or etiquette, which induces me to abstain from reporting the conversation that I overheard. Every American public man, indeed, appears not only to live in a glass house but in a reverberating gallery, and to be absolutely indifferent as to who sees or hears him. This much I may fairly say, that the President asked me several questions about the state of public feeling in England, and obviously, like almost all Americans, was unable to comprehend the causes which have alienated the sympathies of the mother country. At the same time, it struck me that the tone in which he spoke of England was, for an American, unusually fair and candid. There are, perhaps, one or two Lincolniana which I may fairly quote, and which will show the style of his conversation. Some of the party began smoking, and Mr. [William H.] Seward [the secretary of state—ed.], who was present, remarked laughingly, "I have always wondered how any man could ever get to be President of the United States with so few vices. The President, you know, I regret to say, neither drinks nor smokes."

"That," answered the President, "is a doubtful compliment. I recollect once being outside a stage in Illinois, and a man sitting by me offered me a cigar. I told him I had no vices. He said nothing, smoked for some time, and then grunted out, 'It's my experience in life that folks who have got no vices have plaguey few virtues.'"

"The Awkward Bonhommie of His Face"

WILLIAM HOWARD RUSSELL

(1820–1907)

FOREIGN CORRESPONDENT

Russell covered the American war for the *London Times* from 1861 to 1863 and then published a book about his experiences, from which the following recollections are taken. The journalist met Lincoln at a private interview at the White House a few weeks after the inauguration and came away rather startled by the President's appearance and manner. His account begins after he is admitted into "a handsome spacious [White House] room, richly and rather gorgeously furnished," and there waits to be introduced to the chief of state. The recollection resumes the following day when Russell attends a White House reception and gets to hear Lincoln tell one of his famous stories.

Lincoln met Russell again on 14 November 1861, this time in the company of Henry Raymond, editor of *The New York Times*. Their host, Secretary of State Seward, joked, "Here are the two *Times*—if we only get them to do what we want all would go well." To which Lincoln merrily responded: "Yes, if the bad Times would go where we want them, good Times would be sure to follow." ✢

SOON AFTERWARD THERE ENTERED, WITH A SHAMBLING, LOOSE, IRREGULAR, ALMOST UNSTEADY GAIT, A TALL, LANK, LEAN MAN, CONSIDERABLY OVER SIX FEET IN HEIGHT, WITH STOOPING shoulders, long pendulous arms, terminating in hands of extraordinary dimensions, which, however, were far exceeded in proportion by his feet. He was dressed in an ill-fitting, wrinkled suit of black, which put one in mind of an undertaker's uniform at a funeral; round his neck a rope of black silk was knotted in a large bulb, with flying ends projecting beyond the collar of his coat; his turned-down shirt-collar disclosed a sinewy muscular yellow neck, and above that, nestling in a great black mass of hair, bristling and compact like a riff of mourning pins, rose the strange quaint face and head, covered with its thatch of wild republican hair, of President Lincoln. The impression produced by the size of his extremities, and by his flapping and wide projecting ears, may be removed by the appearance of kindliness, sagacity, and the awkward bonhommie of his face; the mouth is absolutely prodigious; the lips, straggling and extending almost from one line of black beard to the other, are only kept in order by two deep furrows from the nostril to the chin; the nose itself—a prominent organ—stands out from the face with an inquiring, anxious air, as though it were sniffing for some good thing in the wind; the eyes dark, full, and deeply set, are penetrating, but full of an expression which almost amounts to tenderness; and above them projects the shaggy brow, running into the small hard frontal space, the development of which can scarcely be estimated accurately, owing to the irregular flocks of thick hair carelessly brushed across it. One would say that, although the mouth was made to enjoy a joke, it could also utter the severest sentence which the head could dictate, but that Mr. Lincoln would be ever more willing to temper justice with mercy, and to enjoy what he considers the amenities of life, than to take a harsh view of men's nature and of the world, and to estimate things in an ascetic or puritan spirit. A person who met Mr. Lincoln in the street would not take him to be what—according to the usages of European society—is called a "gentleman"; and, indeed, since I came to the United States, I have heard more disparaging allusions made by Americans to him on that account than I could have expected among simple republicans, where all should be equals; but at the same time, it would not be possible for the most indifferent observer to pass him in the street without notice.

As he advanced through the room, he evidently controlled a desire to shake hands all round with everybody, and smiled good-humouredly till he was suddenly brought up by the staid deportment of Mr. Seward, and by the profound diplomatic bows of the Chevalier Bertinatti. Then, indeed, he suddenly jerked himself back, and stood in front of the two ministers, with his body slightly drooped forward, and his hands behind his back, his knees touching, and his feet apart. Mr. Seward formally presented the minister, whereupon the President made a prodigiously violent demonstration of his body in a bow which had almost the effect of a smack in its rapidity and abruptness, and, recovering himself, proceeded to give his utmost attention, whilst the Chevalier, with another bow, read from a paper a long address in presenting the royal letter accrediting him as "minister resident"; and when he said that "the king desired to give, under your enlightened administration, all possible strength and extent to those sentiments of frank sympathy which do not cease to be exhibited every moment between the two peoples, and whose origin dates back as far as the exertions which have presided over their common destiny as self-governing and free nations," the President gave another bow still more violent, as much as to accept the allusion.

"He Was the People's Agent"

THE MARQUIS DE CHAMBRUN
(1831–1891)
FOREIGN VISITOR

Charles Adolphe Pineton, the marquis de Chambrun, a titled pro-royalist from France, traveled to America at the end of 1864 and observed Lincoln firsthand in Washington and on the President's final trip to the front in March of 1865, as victory was in sight.

Chambrun recorded his observations in a diary that his daughter preserved. The following impressions of Lincoln come from those letters and from an article published in 1893 in *Scribner's Magazine*. ✤

W E WERE TO LEAVE CITY POINT [THE UNION ARMY HEAD-QUARTERS IN VIRGINIA—ED.] ON SATURDAY, APRIL 8TH. A FEW HOURS PREVIOUS TO DEPARTURE, A MILITARY BAND from Headquarters came on board the *River Queen* [Lincoln's transport—ed.]. After they had given us several pieces, Mr. Lincoln thought of the *Marseillaise,* for which he professed great liking, and asked to have it played. The French anthem was performed a second time; while turning toward me, Mr. Lincoln remarked: "You have to come over to America to hear it" [the anthem was then banned in France—ed.]. He then asked me if I had ever heard the rebel song *Dixie,* to the sound of which all the Southern attacks had been conducted. I replied in the negative. The President continued: "That tune is now Federal property and it is good to show the rebels that, with us in power, they will be free to hear it again." So he told the surprised musicians to play it for us. Thus ended our last evening.

At ten o'clock our boat steamed off. Mr. Lincoln stood a long while gazing at the hills, so animated a few days before, now dark and silent. Around us more than a hundred ships at anchor gave visible proof of the country's maritime strength and testified to the great tasks accomplished.

Mr. Lincoln remained absorbed in thought and pursued his meditation long after the quickened speed had removed the lugubrious scene forever from our sight.

On Sunday, April 9th, we were proceeding up the Potomac. That whole day the conversation turned on literary subjects. Mr. Lincoln read aloud to us for several hours. Most of the passages he selected were from Shakespeare, especially *Macbeth*. The lines after the murder of Duncan, when the new king falls a prey to moral torment, were dramatically dwelt on. Now and then he paused to expatiate on how exact a picture Shakespeare here gives of a murderer's mind when, the dark deed achieved, its perpetrator already envies his victim's calm sleep. He read the scene over twice.

Passing before Mount Vernon, I could not help saying: "Mount Vernon, with its memories of Washington, and Springfield, with those of your own home—revolutionary and civil war—will be equally honored in America." As though awakened from a trance, the President exclaimed: "Springfield, how happy I shall be four years hence to return there in peace and tranquillity."

Our party dispersed on arriving at the Potomac wharf. Mr. and Mrs. Lincoln, Senator [Charles] Sumner [of Massachusetts—ed.] and I drove home in the same carriage. As we drew near Washington, Mrs. Lincoln, who had hitherto remained silently looking at the town, said: "That city is full of enemies." The President, on hearing this, retorted with an impatient gesture: "Enemies, never again must we repeat that word."

When success at last had crowned so many bloody efforts it was impossible to discover in Lincoln any thought of revenge or feeling of bitterness toward the vanquished.

• • •

His early life had left ineffaceable marks upon the former railsplitter, and the powerful President of the United States made no efforts of bad taste to conceal what he had been under or what he had become. That simplicity gave him perfect ease. To be sure, he had not the manners of the world, but he was so perfectly natural that it would have been impossible I shall say not to be surprised at his manners, but to notice them at all.

After a moment's inspection, Mr. Lincoln left with a sort of impression of vague and deep sadness. It is not too much to say that it was rare to converse with him a while without feeling something poignant. Every time I have endeavored to describe this impression, words, nay, the very ideas, have failed me. And, strange to say, Mr. Lincoln was quite humorous, although one could always detect a bit of irony in his humor. He would relate anecdotes, seeking always to bring the point out clearly. He willingly laughed either at what was being said to him or what he said himself. But all of a sudden he would retire within himself; then he would close his eyes, and all his features would at once bespeak a kind of sadness as indescribable as it was deep. After a while, as though it were by an effort of his will, he would shake off this mysterious weight under which he seemed bowed; his generous and open disposition would again reappear. In one evening I happened to count over twenty of these alternations and contrasts.

Anyone hearing him express his ideas, or think aloud, either upon one of the great topics which absorbed him, or on an incidental question, was not long in finding out the marvelous rectitude of his mind, nor the accuracy of his judgment. I have heard him give his opinion on statesmen, argue political problems, always with astounding precision and justness. I have heard him speak of a woman who was considered beautiful, discuss the particular character of her appearance, distinguish what was praiseworthy from what was open to criticism, all that with the sagacity of the artist. . . .

It would not be true to say that he was a man gifted with creative faculties; he was not one of those rare and terrible geniuses who, being once possessed of an idea, apply it, curbing and sacrificing other men to the imperious instinct of their will. No; but, on the other hand, he knew better than anyone the exact will of the American people. Amid the noisy confusion of discordant voices which always arises in a free country at moments of crises he would distinguish with marvelous acuteness the true voice of public opinion. He had, however, nothing in common with these politicians, ever on the track of what seems to them to be popular caprice. His firm will, his exalted nature, above all, his inflexible honesty, always kept him aloof from those lamentable schemes; yet he well understood that he was the people's agent, and that his duty obliged him to stand by his principle; for he was well aware of that close union which must exist in a free democracy between the authority representing the nation and the nation itself.

6. MEMORIES FROM FOES

Post–Civil War memoirists, given traditionally to stirring the embers of the glowing Lincoln legend, almost universally heaped on the martyred hero the kind of accolades he seldom received while he lived. The record might have been more balanced, indeed more compelling, had, say, Lincoln's lifelong rival in politics, Stephen A. Douglas, lived long enough to write his own autobiography. But Douglas, whose jibes at Lincoln during their 1858 campaign debates were cruel and biting, died in the first year of Lincoln's presidency, and we will never know for sure how he regarded his longtime foe. Even though Douglas might have been tempted later to celebrate, not criticize. One does not subject saints to attack.

Only a few exceptions to this rule grace the literature. In the measured reminiscences of Confederate vice president Alexander H. Stephens, for example, who had served alongside Lincoln as a fellow Whig congressman in the late 1840s, a modern reader can find some profound, if subtle, criticism: Lincoln, Stephens implied, was simply too stubborn for his own—or the country's—good.

As for Gen. George B. McClellan, the hesitant Union comman-der who challenged Lincoln for reelection in 1864, he did little, in his private letters to his wife from the front, to disguise an almost patho-logical hatred for the President. Here, extrapolated from those letters, are a series of brief denunciations that add up to a sharply critical view of a leader he regarded contemptuously as a "gorilla."

It is a shame that more such frank, if overwrought, condemna-tions do not survive. Lincoln's heroic death inured him from chal-lenges to his martyr-of-liberty image. The exceptions are, in their way, priceless reminders that Lincoln was once a highly controversial, deeply doubted public figure. ✣

"The President Is an Idiot"

GEORGE B. MCCLELLAN

(1826–1885)

UNION GENERAL

West Point–trained, gallant in the field, and inspiring in military reviews, McClellan possessed all the tools required by a successful commander except one: a willingness to attack the enemy. Lincoln appointed him commander in chief of the army of the Potomac at the age of thirty-five, and McClellan successfully restored fighting spirit to troops demoralized after the Union defeat at Bull Run. But his 1862 campaign offensive against the Confederate capital of Richmond foundered on the Virginia Peninsula, as McClellan fretted about the size of enemy forces. Nor was his victory over Robert E. Lee at Antietam that September as decisive as it might have been.

McClellan also treated Lincoln with considerable disrespect, ignoring him once in his own home, and on another occasion presumptuously advising the President on the issue of emancipation, which the general opposed. Frustrated with McClellan's "slows," Lincoln dismissed him in November 1862. "Little Mac's" unflattering views about his commander in chief are extracted from letters he wrote to his wife from the field, in which he did not conceal his contempt. ✣

[16 August 1861]: The President is an idiot. . . .

[c. 11 October 1861]: The President is nothing more than a well meaning baboon.

[17 November 1861]: I went to the White House shortly after tea where I found "the *original gorilla,*" about as intelligent as ever. What a specimen to be at the head of our affairs now!

[21 November 1861]: Herr Hermann, "a great Magician," volunteered to give us a private entertainment, so I invited all the staff etc. [to] it. The most striking feature of the performance was that the Magician asked the President for his handkerchief—upon which the dignitary replied promptly, "You've got me now, I ain't got any"!!!!

[8 April 1862]: The President very coolly telegraphed me yesterday that he thought I had better break the enemy's lines at once! I was much tempted to reply that he had better come and do it himself.

[22 June 1862]: That Honest A[be] has again fallen into the hands of my enemies and is no longer a cordial friend of mine. . . . I tremble for my country when I think of these things.

[10 July 1862]: I do not know what paltry trick the Administration will play next—I did not like the President's manner—it seemed that of a man about to do something of which he was much ashamed.

[29 October 1862]: If you could know the mean and dirty character of the dispatches I receive you would boil over with anger—when it is possible to misunderstand, and when it is not possible, whenever there is a chance of a wretched innuendo—there it comes. But the good of the country requires me to submit to all this from men whom I know to be greatly my inferiors socially, intellectually and morally! There never was a truer epithet applied to a certain individual than that of the "Gorilla."

"Mr. Lincoln Does Not Have Character"

STEPHEN A. DOUGLAS
(1813–1861)
POLITICAL RIVAL

"The Little Giant" was "Long Abe's" lifetime rival in Illinois and national politics. As lawyers, the two men occasionally opposed each other in court; as politicians, they debated national issues as early as 1840—eighteen years before their celebrated Senate debates helped elevate Lincoln's national reputation.

"Two men presenting wider contrasts," a New York journalist reported, "could hardly be found: . . . [Douglas,] a short, thick-set, burly man . . . proud, defiant, arrogant, audacious, [and Lincoln,] the opposite . . . tall, slender and angular, awkward even, in gait and attitude." Douglas became a congressman, then a United States senator from Illinois. According to legend, he was once also Lincoln's rival for the hand of Springfield belle Mary Todd. Mary admitted only that Douglas had been one of the "choice spirits" of her "drawing room."

The two men made peace after Lincoln was elected President. Douglas held Lincoln's hat in a symbolic gesture of unity at the 1861 inaugural and embarked on a speaking tour to oppose secession. He died that June, and Lincoln ordered the White House draped in black in tribute.

Douglas made the following sarcastic, tongue-in-cheek assessment of his foe's career and character during their first joint Senate debate in Ottawa, Illinois, on 21 August 1858. ✤

I N THE REMARKS WHICH I HAVE MADE UPON THIS PLATFORM, AND THE POSITIONS OF MR. LINCOLN UPON IT, I MEAN NOTHING PERSONAL, DISRESPECTFUL, OR UNKIND TO THAT GENTLEMAN. I have known him for nearly twenty-five years. We had many points of sympathy when I first got acquainted with him. We were both comparatively boys—both struggling with poverty in a strange land for our support. I an humble school teacher in the town of Winchester, and he a flourishing grocery [in frontier parlance, a saloon—ed.] keeper in the town of [New] Salem. He was more successful than I, and thus became more fortunate in this world's goods. Mr. Lincoln is one of those peculiar men that has performed with admirable skill in every occupation that he ever attempted. I made as good a school teacher as I could, and when a cabinet maker I made the best bedsteads and tables, but my old bones said I succeeded better in bureaus and secretaries than in anything else. But I believe that Mr. Lincoln was more successful in his business than I, for his business soon carried him directly into the Legislature. There I met him in a little time, and I had a sympathy for him, because of the up hill struggle that we had in life. He was then as good at telling an anecdote as now. He could beat any of the boys at wrestling—could outrun them at a foot race—beat them at pitching quoits and tossing a copper, and could win more liquor than all the boys put together; and the dignity and impartiality with which he presided at a horse-race or fist-fight were the praise of everybody that was present and participated. Hence I had sympathy for him, because he was struggling with misfortune and so was I.

Mr. Lincoln served with me, or I with him, in the Legislature of 1836, when we parted. He subsided or submerged for some years, and I lost sight of him. In 1846, when [David] Wilmot [Pennsylvania senator, ed.] raised the Wilmot Proviso tornado [a failed but portentous 1846 attempt to bar slavery from territory captured in the Mexican war—ed.], Mr. Lincoln again turned up as a member of Congress from Sangamon District. I, being in the Senate of the United States, was called to welcome him, then without friend and companion. He then distinguished himself by his opposition to the Mexican war, taking the side of the common enemy, in time of war, against his own country. When he returned home from that Congress, he found that the indignation of the people followed him everywhere, until he again retired to private life, and was submerged until he was forgotten again by his friends. He came up again in 1854, just in time to make the

Abolition–Black Republican platform, in company with [fellow Republicans] Lovejoy, Giddings, Chase, and Fred[erick]. Douglass, for the Republican party to stand upon. . . .

I do not question Mr. Lincoln's conscientious belief that the negro was made his equal, and hence is his brother. But, for my own part, I do not regard the Negro as my equal, and I positively deny that he is my brother, or any kin to me whatever. But he [Lincoln] . . . holds that the negro was endowed with equality by the Almighty, and hence that no human power alone can deprive him of these rights which the Almighty has guaranteed to him. . . .

I have not brought a charge of moral turpitude against him, and when he or any other living man brings one against me, instead of putting myself on the proof and disproving it, I will say it is a lie! . . .

Mr. Lincoln does not have character enough for integrity and truth.

"He Had a Native Genius"

—◆◈◆—

ALEXANDER H. STEPHENS

(1812–1883)

VICE PRESIDENT OF THE CONFEDERACY

Lincoln met Stephens when both men were serving as congressmen in 1847. Lincoln admired the "little slim, pale-faced man" from Georgia, writing home to admit that one of Stephens's speeches from the floor of the House of Representatives had reduced him to tears. Although

Stephens initially opposed secession, he pledged his allegiance to the South when his state left the Union, and he was elected vice president of the new Confederate States of America.

Stephens wrote somewhat disparagingly of Lincoln in his 1870 book, *Constitutional View of the Late War between the States*. The unreconstructed Rebel was kinder when he spoke at the United States Capitol on Lincoln's birthday, 1878, at the unveiling of Francis B. Carpenter's painting of *The First Reading of the Emancipation Proclamation before the Cabinet*. The second excerpt comes from this conciliatory address. The third and final comments are drawn from Stephens's brief 1881 tribute to Lincoln in the collection, *The Lincoln Memorial*. ✢

———◆◆◆◆———

I DO NOT THINK THAT HE INTENDED TO OVERTHROW THE INSTITUTIONS OF THE COUNTRY. I DO NOT THINK HE UNDERSTOOD THEM OR THE TENDENCIES OF HIS ACTS UPON THEM. THE UNION with him in sentiment, rose to the sublimity of a religious mysticism, while his ideas of its structure and formation in logic, rested upon nothing but the subtleties of a sophism!

I knew Mr. Lincoln well. We met in the House in December, 1847. We were together during the Thirtieth Congress. I was as intimate with him as with any other man of that Congress, except perhaps one. That exception was my colleague, Mr. [Robert] Toombs [a fellow Georgian, and later a Confederate cabinet minister—ed.]. Of Mr. Lincoln's general character I need not speak. He was warm-hearted; he was generous; he was magnanimous; he was most truly, as he afterward said on a memorable occasion, "with malice toward none, with charity for all."

In bodily form he was above the average, and so in intellect; the two were in symmetry. Not highly cultivated, he had a native genius far above the average of his fellows. Every fountain of his heart was ever overflowing with the "milk of human kindness." So much for him personally. From my attachment to him, so much the deeper was the pang in my own breast as well as of millions at the horrible manner of "his taking off" [a quote from *Macbeth*—ed.]. That was the climax of our troubles and the spring from which came afterward "unnumbered woes." But of those events no more now. Widely as we differed on public questions and policies, yet as a friend I may say:

> No farther seek his merits to disclose,
> Or draw his frailties from their dread abode;
> There they alike in trembling hope repose,
> The bosom of his Father and his God.

Mr. Lincoln was careful as to his manners, awkward in his speech, but was possessed of a very strong, clear and vigorous mind. He always attracted the riveted attention of the House when he spoke; his manner of speech as well as thought was original. He had no model. He was a man of strong convictions, and was what Carlyle would have called an earnest man. He abounded in anecdotes; he illustrated everything that he was talking or speaking about by an anecdote; his anecdotes were always exceedingly apt and pointed, and socially he always kept his company in a roar of laughter.

"A Disgrace to the Seat He Holds"

JOHN WILKES BOOTH

(1838–1865)

ACTOR, ASSASSIN

Born in Maryland to a famous acting family, Booth, a matinee idol before he was twenty-five, was particularly renowned for his athletic leaps on stage. He was also an unreconstructible white supremacist, and he developed an intense hatred for Lincoln, blaming him for threatening slavery in Booth's native Maryland and for refusing to allow the pro-slavery Confederate states to secede without a fight.

Sometime in 1864 he organized a plan to kidnap Lincoln and ransom him for the exchange of Confederate prisoners of war. The plot failed, and when the war ended Booth decided instead to exact revenge and kill the President. He pulled the trigger of his pistol on 14 April 1865. Whether or not Booth was a professional Confederate agent on official assignment to eliminate the enemy commander in chief, or a racist fanatic determined to avenge the South, remains the subject of lively historical debate. What we know is that he was among the crowd on the White House lawn to hear Lincoln give his last speech. Reportedly, Booth was so outraged when the President raised the issue of extending to African-American veterans the right to vote, he seethed: "That means nigger equality. Now by God! I'll put him through. That is the last speech he will ever make."

Booth's vitriolic views about Lincoln are taken here from his sister Asia's memoir, written in 1938. She recollects a portion of conversation she had with the future assassin. The second entry comes from a letter Booth prepared for the *National Intelligencer* just hours before he killed the President. ✤

━━━◆◆◆━━━

THAT SECTIONAL CANDIDATE SHOULD NEVER HAVE BEEN PRESIDENT, THE VOTES WERE *DOUBLED* TO SEAT HIM, HE WAS SMUGGLED THROUGH MARYLAND TO THE WHITE HOUSE. . . . This man's appearance, his pedigree, his coarse low jokes and anecdotes, his vulgar similes, and his frivolity, are a disgrace to the seat he holds. Other brains rule the country. *He* is made the tool of the North, to crush out, or try to crush out slavery, by robbery, rapine, slaughter and bought armies. He is walking in the footprints of Old John Brown, but no more fit to stand with that rugged old hero—Great God! no. John Brown was a man inspired by the grandest character of the century! *He* is a Bonaparte in one great move, that is, by overturning this blind Republic and making himself a king. This man's re-election which will follow his success, I tell you—will be a reign! The subjects—bastard subjects—of other countries, apostates, are eager to overturn this government. You'll see—you'll see—that *re-election* means succession. . . . by a half-breed too, a man springing from the ashes of old ["Osawatomie" John] Brown, a false president yearning for kingly succession as hotly as ever did Ariston.

Many, I know—the vulgar herd—will blame me for what I am about to do, but posterity, I am sure, will justify me. Right or wrong, God judge me, not man. . . . This war is a war with the constitution and the reserve rights of the state. It is a war upon Southern rights and institutions. The nomination of Abraham Lincoln four years ago bespoke war. His election forced it. I have ever held the South were right. . . .

People of the North, to hate tyranny and to love liberty and justice, to strike at wrong and oppression, was the teaching of our fathers. The study of our early history will not let me forget it, and may it never.

I do not want to forget the heroic patriotism of our fathers, who rebelled against the oppression of the mother country.

This country was formed for the white, not for the black man.

7. MEMORIES FROM MILITARY MEN

By the time Lincoln became president, few Americans remembered that he had earlier been an anti-war congressman who once rose on the House floor to question "the exceeding brightness of military glory—that attractive rainbow, that rises in showers of blood." Less than fifteen years later he was commander in chief of the largest army the world had ever known. He instituted a military draft, encouraged the enlistment of the first African-American regiments in the service, approved an income tax to pay for the military, and rallied the Union to wage a bloody war to prevent its dissolution.

It could not have been an easy transition. Lincoln's Confederate counterpart, Jefferson Davis, was a West Point–trained Mexican War hero and a former U.S. secretary of war. Lincoln's sole military experience had come in a small frontier Indian conflict in which the only "bloody struggles" he could recall had been waged against "the mesquetoes."

Early in his term, a stranger was moved to complain to Lincoln after observing him reviewing a regiment of troops: "A lawyer in his office can put his feet on a table higher than his head, if he wishes to, but he cant come [*sic*] any such performance as Commander in Chief. . . . You need more dignity."

Dignity—and an astonishing skill for handling officers and planning strategy—is just what Lincoln developed. Immersing himself in the classics of military literature, he taught himself the elements of planning battles. Learning from his own mistakes when he appointed ineffective commanders, he began choosing men more wisely. Somehow he transformed himself into a better strategist "than any of his generals," in the words of one noted Civil War historian, and "did more than Grant or any general to win the war for the Union." From his military family Lincoln demanded "energy, and sleepless vigilance."

Over time, most of his professional commanders developed broad respect and intense loyalty for Lincoln, as many of the following reminiscences remind us. Even hardened soldiers like Grant and Sherman observed him with awe and remembered him with affection.

In the following selections, Lincoln is recalled as a frequent visitor to army outposts, encouraging action, greeting soldiers, and making clear how he wanted the war to be prosecuted. With his familiar black frock coat and top hat, Lincoln may have seemed the quintessential civilian. But as these recollections demonstrate, he was also every inch the commander in chief. The "army dominates all the country," Lincoln declared in 1863, "and all the people, within its range." And Lincoln, in turn, dominated the army. ✤

"He Never Stepped Too Soon"

CHARLES A. DANA

(1819–1897)

ASSISTANT SECRETARY OF WAR

When the Civil War began, Dana was serving as managing editor of the pro-Republican *New York Tribune,* where he had worked since 1847. But he joined the War Department in 1862, and rose to the post of Assistant Secretary the following year. Three years after the end of the Rebellion, Dana purchased the New York *Sun,* which he owned and operated for the next 29 years, becoming one of the nation's most influential newspapermen. But despite his considerable firsthand experiences and editorial expertise, Dana appeared unable to assemble his wartime reminiscences until author Ida Tarbell conducted extensive interviews, and essentially ghost-wrote his memoir. It is from this book, *Recollections of the Civil War with the Leaders at Washington and in the Field in the Sixties,* published posthumously, that the following recollections of Lincoln are drawn. ✛

LINCOLN HAD THE MOST COMPREHENSIVE, THE MOST JUDICIOUS MIND; HE WAS THE LEAST FAULTY IN HIS CONCLUSIONS OF ANY MAN I HAVE EVER KNOWN. HE NEVER STEPPED TOO soon, and he never stepped too late. When the whole Northern country seemed to be clamoring for him to issue a proclamation abolishing slavery, he didn't do it. Deputation after deputation went to Washington. I remember once a hundred gentlemen, dressed in black coats, mostly clergymen, from Massachusetts, came to Washington to appeal to him to proclaim the abolition of slavery. But he did not do it. He allowed Mr. Cameron and General Butler to execute their great idea of treating slaves as contraband of war and protecting those who had got into our lines against being recaptured by their Southern owners; but he would not prematurely make the proclamation that was so much desired. Finally the time came, and of that he was the judge. Nobody else decided it; nobody commanded it; the proclamation was issued as he thought best, and it was efficacious. The people of the North, who during the long contest over slavery had always stood strenuously by the compromises of the Constitution, might themselves have become half rebels if this proclamation had been issued too soon. At last they were tired of waiting, tired of endeavoring to preserve even a show of regard for what was called "the compromises of the Constitution" when they believed the Constitution itself was in danger. Thus public opinion was ripe when the proclamation came, and that was the beginning of the end. He could have issued this proclamation two years before, perhaps, and the consequence of it might have been our entire defeat; but when it came it did its work, and it did us no harm whatever. Nobody protested against it, not even the Confederates themselves.

This unerring judgment, this patience which waited and which knew when the right time had arrived, is an intellectual quality that I do not find exercised upon any such scale and with such absolute precision by any other man in history. It proves Abraham Lincoln to have been intellectually one of the greatest of rulers. If we look through the record of great men, where is there one to be placed beside him? I do not know.

. . . Another interesting fact about Abraham Lincoln is that he developed into a great military man; that is to say, a man of supreme military judgment. I do not risk anything in saying that if one will study the records of the war and study the writings relating to it, he will agree with me that the greatest general we had, greater than Grant or Thomas, was Abraham Lincoln. It was not so at the beginning; but after three or four years of constant practice in the science and art of war, he arrived at this extraordinary knowledge of it, so that Von Moltke was not a better general, or an abler planner or expounder of a campaign, than was President Lincoln. To sum it up, he was a born leader of men. He knew human nature; he knew what chord to strike, and was never afraid to strike it when he believed that the time had arrived.

Another remarkable quality of Mr. Lincoln was his great mercifulness. A thing it seemed as if he could not do was to sign a death warrant. One day General Augur, who was the major general commanding the forces in and around Washington, came to my office and said:

"Here is So-and-So, a spy. He has been tried by court-martial; the facts are perfectly established, he has been sentenced to death, and here is the warrant for his execution, which is fixed for tomorrow morning at six o'clock. The President is away. If he were here, the man certainly wouldn't be executed. He isn't here. I think it very essential to the safety of the service and the safety of everything that an example should be made of this spy. They do us great mischief; and it is very important that the law which all nations recognize in dealing with spies, and the punishment which every nation assigns to them, should be inflicted upon at least one of these wretches who haunt us around Washington. Do you know whether the President will be back before morning?"

"I understand that he won't be back until tomorrow afternoon," I replied.

"Well, as the President is not here, will you sign the warrant?"

"Go to Mr. Stanton," I said; "he is the authority."

"I have been to him, and he said I should come to you."

Well, I signed the order; I agreed with General Augur in his view of the question. At about eleven o'clock the next day I met the general. "The President got home at two o'clock this morning," he said, "and he stopped it all."

"Evidence of a Wisdom and Purity"

◆━━◆◆◆━━◆

E. W. ANDREWS

(1812–?)

MINISTER, LAWYER, SOLDIER

Trained first in carriagemaking, then in the law, Andrews became a Congregationalist minister, serving in various parishes in Connecticut and New York before resuming his career at the bar.

When the Rebellion broke out, he organized Union troops in Westchester and Rockland Counties in New York and ultimately became chief of staff to Gen. W. W. Morris, stationed near Baltimore. Morris was unable to accept an invitation to meet and accompany President Lincoln's train to Gettysburg for the dedication of the Soldiers' National Cemetery in November 1863, so Andrews went instead—and there got to witness Lincoln's oratorical zenith, the Gettysburg Address, which he recalled twenty-five years later for editor Allen Thorndike Rice's *Reminiscences of Lincoln by Distinguished Men of his Time.* ✛

THE NATIONAL CEMETERY AT GETTYSBURG WAS DEDICATED ON THE 17TH OF NOVEMBER, 1863. SHORTLY BEFORE THE DEDICATION WAS TO TAKE PLACE THE PRESIDENT SENT AN INVITATION to my chief, General W. W. Morris, and his staff, to join him at Baltimore and accompany him on his special train to Gettysburg. General Morris was sick at the time, and requested me, as his chief of staff, to represent him on that occasion. The General was suffering from one of the troubles which tried the patience of Job.

On the day appointed, therefore, I presented myself, with two other members of the staff, to President Lincoln, on his arrival at Baltimore, and offered the apology of my chief for his absence.

After cordially greeting us and directing us to make ourselves comfortable, the President, with quizzical expression, turned to Montgomery Blair (then Postmaster-General), and said:

"Blair, did you ever know that fright has sometimes proved a sure cure for boils?"

"No, Mr. President. How is that?"

"I'll tell you. Not long ago, when Colonel ———, with his cavalry, was at the front, and the Rebs were making things rather lively for us, the colonel was ordered out on a *reconnaissance*. He was troubled at the time with a big boil where it made horseback riding decidedly uncomfortable. He hadn't gone more than two or three miles when he declared he couldn't stand it any longer, and dismounted and ordered the troops forward without him. He had just settled down to enjoy his relief from change of position when he was startled by the rapid reports of pistols and the helter-skelter approach of his troops in full retreat before a yelling rebel force. He forgot everything but the yells, sprang into his saddle, and made capital time over fences and ditches till safe within the lines. The pain from his boil was gone, and the boil too, and the colonel swore that there was no cure for boils so sure as fright from rebel yells, and that the secession had rendered to loyalty *one* valuable service at any rate."

During the ride to Gettysburg the President placed every one who approached him at his ease, relating numerous stories, some of them laughable, and others of a character that deeply touched the hearts of his listeners. . . .

Around the platform, on which the addresses were delivered, the military were formed in hollow square several ranks deep. Inside of this square, and but a few feet from the platform, I had my position, and thus enjoyed the best opportunities to see and hear. . . .

At length, and in the name of the American Republic, the President came forward formally to dedicate the place, which had drank so freely of the life-blood of her sons, as their peaceful resting-place till time should be no more, pledging the fidelity and honor and power of the government to its preservation for this sacred purpose while that government should last.

A description of the President's famous address is needless; it has already become a classic; it is impossible to conceive of anything more beautiful and appropriate for the occasion.

But I may say a word of the appearance of the orator.

President Lincoln was so put together physically that, to him, gracefulness of movement was an impossibility. But his awkwardness was lost sight of in the interest which the expression of his face and what he said awakened.

On this occasion he came out before the vast assembly, and stepped slowly to the front of the platform, with his hands clasped before him, his natural sadness of expression deepened, his head bent forward, and his eyes cast to the ground.

In this attitude he stood for a few seconds, silent, as if communing with his own thoughts; and when he began to speak, and throughout his entire address, his manner indicated no consciousness of the presence of tens of thousands hanging on his lips, but rather of one who, like the prophet of old, was overmastered by some unseen spirit of the scene, and passively gave utterance to the memories, the feelings, the counsels and the prophecies with which he was inspired.

In his whole appearance, as well as in his wonderful utterances, there was such evidence of a wisdom and purity and benevolence and moral grandeur, higher and beyond the reach of ordinary men, that the great assembly listened almost awe-struck as to a voice from the divine oracle.

"Impressed by His Kindly Nature"

WILLIAM TECUMSEH SHERMAN
(1820–1891)
UNION GENERAL

After a rocky start as a Union commander in Kentucky, where he was dogged by rumors of a mental breakdown, Sherman went on to considerable glory—and controversy—emerging as the principal Union military leader in the West. He took Atlanta in September of 1864 and then led his army on a daring, devastating march through Georgia, culminating with the conquest of Savannah at Christmastime.

As the Rebellion withered, Sherman joined Grant and Adm. David Dixon Porter for a final meeting with Lincoln on board the steamer *River Queen* at City Point, Virginia, on 27–28 March 1865. Sherman insisted in his *Memoirs*—from which this reminiscence is drawn—that Lincoln made it clear at the conference that he wanted the war to end without retribution. Some historians have since challenged Sherman's recollections, but there is little reason to believe that the general would have so grossly misinterpreted the President's intentions.

Sherman's are still the most valuable insights into Lincoln's last "council of war." They reveal a commander in chief magnanimous in the face of imminent victory. Earlier in the month, he had called in his inaugural address for "malice toward none." As Sherman recalled it, Lincoln fully intended to practice what he preached. ✢

W E WALKED DOWN TO THE WHARF, WENT ON BOARD, AND FOUND MR. LINCOLN ALONE, IN THE AFTER-CABIN. HE RE-MEMBERED ME PERFECTLY, AND AT ONCE ENGAGED IN A most interesting conversation. He was full of curiosity about the many incidents of our great march, which had reached him officially and through the newspapers, and seemed to enjoy very much the most ludicrous parts—about the "bummers," and their devices to collect food and forage when the outside world supposed us to be starving; but at the same time he expressed a good deal of anxiety lest some accident might happen to the army in North Carolina during my absence. . . .

Both General Grant and myself supposed that one or the other of us would have to fight one more bloody battle, and that it would be the *last*. Mr. Lincoln exclaimed, more than once, that there had been blood enough shed, and asked us if another battle could not be avoided. I remember well to have said that we could not control that event; that this necessarily rested with our enemy; and I inferred that both Jefferson Davis and General Lee would be forced to fight one more desperate and bloody battle. I rather supposed it would fall on me, somewhere near Raleigh; and General Grant added that, if Lee would only wait a few more days, he would have his army so disposed that if the enemy should abandon Richmond, and attempt to make junction with General Joseph Johnston in North Carolina, he (General Grant) would be on his heels. Mr. Lincoln more than once expressed uneasiness that I was not with my army at Goldsboro', when I again assured him that General [John M.] Schofield was fully competent to command in my absence; that I was going to start back that very day, and that Admiral Porter had kindly provided for me the steamer *Bat,* which he said was much swifter than my own vessel, the *Russia.* During this interview I inquired of the President if he was all ready for the end of the war. What was to be done with the rebel armies when defeated? And what should be done with the political leaders, such as Jefferson Davis, etc.? Should we allow them to escape, etc.? He said he was all ready; all he wanted of us was to defeat the opposing armies, and to get the men composing the Confederate armies back to their homes, at work on their farms and in their shops. As to Jefferson Davis, he was hardly at liberty to speak his mind fully, but intimated that he ought to clear out, "escape the country," only it would not do for him to say so openly. As usual, he illustrated his meaning by a story: "A man once had taken the total-abstinence pledge. When visiting a friend, he was invited to take a drink, but declined, on the score of his pledge, when his friend suggested lemon-ade, which was accepted. In preparing the lemonade, the friend pointed to the brandy-bottle, and said the lemonade would be more palatable if he were to pour in a little brandy; when his guest said, if he could do so 'unbeknown' to him, he would not object." From which illustration I inferred that Mr. Lincoln wanted Davis to escape, "un-beknown" to him. . . .

I know, when I left him, that I was more than ever impressed by his kindly nature, his deep and earnest sympathy with the afflictions of the whole people, resulting from the war, and by the march of hostile armies through the South; and that his earnest desire seemed to be to end the war speedily, without more bloodshed or devastation, and to restore all the men of both sections to their homes. In the language of his second inaugural address, he seemed to have "charity for all, mal-ice toward none," and, above all, an absolute faith in the courage, manliness, and integrity of the armies in the field. When at rest or lis-tening, his legs and arms seemed to hang almost lifeless, and his face was care-worn and haggard; but, the moment he began to talk, his face lightened up, his tall form, as it were, unfolded, and he was the very impersonation of good-humor and fellowship. The last words I recall as addressed to me were that he would feel better when I was back at Goldsboro'. We parted at the gangway of the *River Queen*, about noon of March 28, and I never saw him again. Of all the men I ever met, he seemed to possess more of the elements of greatness, combined with goodness, than any other.

"Never Professed to Be a Military Man"

ULYSSES S. GRANT

(1822–1885)

UNION GENERAL

Grant did not set eyes on Lincoln until the general had become a Union war hero and was summoned to Washington to receive command of all the Federal armies with the exalted rank of lieutenant general. On 9 March 1864, the President hosted a White House reception for the general, conveying to Grant, in his remarks, "the nation's appreciation of what you have done," and adding: "I scarcely need to add that with what I here speak for the nation goes my own hearty personal concurrence." Grant in turn remained a warm supporter of the President, grateful and "astonished," as he put it in a letter to Lincoln a few months later, "at the readiness which every thin[g] asked for has been yielded without even an explanation being asked."

Grant was himself swept into the presidency in an 1868 landslide and served two terms, the second marred by scandal, which hardly reduced the old general's personal popularity. He became a global celebrity and an American icon, but by the time he learned he was suffering from incurable cancer his finances were in ruins. Determined to provide security for his family, he heroically set about writing an autobiography, which he completed, despite great physical pain, just before his death. It became a huge posthumous bestseller.

The first of the following reminiscences is taken from that memoir; the second consists of anecdotes that the general included in the first draft of the book, but later deleted. His son, Frederick, provided them to Allen Thorndike Rice for his 1888 compendium, *Reminiscences of Lincoln by Distinguished Men of His Time*. ✣

⤙━◆◆◆━⤚

ALTHOUGH HAILING FROM ILLINOIS MYSELF, THE STATE OF THE PRESIDENT, I NEVER MET MR. LINCOLN UNTIL CALLED TO THE CAPITAL TO RECEIVE MY COMMISSION AS LIEUTENANT-general. I knew him, however, very well and favorably from the accounts given by officers under me at the West who had known him all their lives. I had also read the remarkable series of debates between Lincoln and Douglas a few years before, when they were rival candidates for the United States Senate. I was then a resident of Missouri, and by no means a "Lincoln man" in that contest; but I recognized then his great ability.

In my first interview with Mr. Lincoln alone he stated to me that he had never professed to be a military man or to know how campaigns should be conducted, and never wanted to interfere in them; but that procrastination on the part of commanders, and the pressure from the people at the North and from Congress, *which was always with him,* forced him into issuing his series of "Military Orders"—No. 1, No. 2, No. 3, etc. He did not know that they were not all wrong, and did know that some of them were. All he wanted, or had ever wanted, was some one who would take the responsibility and act and call on him for all the assistance needed; he would pledge himself to use all the power of the Government in rendering such assistance. Assuring him that I would do the best I could with the means at hand, and avoid as far as possible annoying him or the War Department, our first interview ended.

Just after receiving my commission as lieutenant-general, the President called me aside to speak to me privately. After a brief reference to the military situation, he said he thought he could illustrate what he wanted to say by a story, which he related as follows: "At one time there was a great war among the animals, and one side had great difficulty in getting a commander who had sufficient confidence in himself. Finally, they found a monkey, by the name of Jocko, who said that he thought he could command their army if his tail could be made a little longer. So they got more tail and spliced it on to his caudal appendage. He looked at it admiringly, and then thought he ought to have a little more still. This was added, and again he called for more. The splicing process was repeated many times, until they had coiled Jocko's tail around the room, filling all the space. Still he called for more tail, and, there being no other place to coil it, they began wrapping it around his shoulders. He continued his call for more, and they kept on winding the additional tail about him until its weight broke him down."

I saw the point, and, rising from my chair, replied: "Mr. President, I will not call for more assistance unless I find it impossible to do with what I already have. . . ."

Upon one occasion, when the President was at my head-quarters at City Point, I took him to see the work that had been done on the Dutch Gap Canal. After taking him around and showing him all the points of interest, explaining how, in blowing up one portion of the work that was being excavated, the explosion had thrown the material back into, and filled up, a part already completed, he turned to me and said: "Grant, do you know what this reminds me of? Out in Springfield, Illinois, there was a blacksmith named ———. One day, when he did not have much to do, he took a piece of soft iron that had been in his shop for some time, and for which he had no special use, and, starting up his fire, began to heat it. When he got it hot he carried it to the anvil and began to hammer it, rather thinking he would weld it into an agricultural implement. He pounded away for some time until he got it fashioned into some shape, when he discovered that the iron would not hold out to complete the implement he had in mind. He then put it back into the forge, heated it up again, and recommenced hammering, with an ill-defined notion that he would make a claw hammer, but after a time he came to the conclusion that there was more iron there than was needed to form a hammer. Again he heated it, and thought he would make an axe. After hammering and welding it into shape, knocking the oxydized iron off in flakes, he concluded there was not enough of the iron left to make an axe that would be of any use. He was now getting tired and a little disgusted at the result of his various essays. So he filled his forge full of coal, and, after placing the iron in the center of the heap, took the bellows and worked up a tremendous blast, bringing the iron to a white heat. Then with his tongs he lifted it from the bed of coals, and thrusting it into a tub of water near by, exclaimed with an oath, 'Well, if I can't make anything else of you, I will make a fizzle, anyhow.'"

I replied that I was afraid that was about what we had done with the Dutch Gap Canal.

8. MEMORIES FROM AUTHORS

Lincoln's intense passion for reading has become the stuff of legend. And on this subject, legend and fact agree. Lincoln was an avid reader who remembered whole passages, soliloquies, and poems. He memorized parts of the Bible, and nearly all the poetry of Robert Burns—even as he was studying law. He read Shakespeare, he once contended, "perhaps as frequently as any unprofessional reader." And he once startled two eyewitnesses by reciting entirely from memory a long and maudlin poem by the little-known William Knox. He had cut out a newspaper reprint of the verses and had carried it in his pocket, he proudly told them, "until I had it by heart."

On the other hand, notwithstanding early testimony that he may have taken up *Pilgrim's Progress* and *Robinson Crusoe* as a young man, there is no hard evidence that Lincoln ever read a novel from cover to cover in his entire life. Lincoln earned the respect of many of the writers of his own time, novelists among them, not for his reading, but for his writing. Harriet Beecher Stowe, for one, thought there were "passages in his state-papers . . . worthy to be inscribed in letters of gold." (Yet, it seems possible that Lincoln never read Stowe's most enduring work, the highly influential *Uncle Tom's Cabin*.)

Stowe was not Lincoln's only admirer. Poet Walt Whitman so adored the president that he recalled each of his sightings of Lincoln as if they were reunions with an intimate friend. And the preeminent historian George Bancroft admired his "good common sense, his shrewd sagacity . . . his rare combination of fixedness and pliancy." Meeting the writer for the first time on a White House receiving line, Lincoln recognized him and exclaimed happily: "Hold on—I know you; you are—History, History of the United States, Mr.—Mr. Bancroft, Mr. George Bancroft." Lincoln had evidently read this long nonfiction work as well.

Bancroft was a Democrat in politics, as was Nathaniel Hawthorne, who had occasion once to meet Lincoln at the White House. The novelist's forthright recollection of that interview seemed so daring at the time that it was censored after he prepared it for publication. Today, when readers are more familiar with Lincoln's homey virtues than with the stiff dignity his supporters thought essential to his reputation, Hawthorne's descriptions hardly sound disrespectful. In fact, they have the ring of truth. ✦

"The Homeliest Man I Ever Saw"

NATHANIEL HAWTHORNE

(1804–1864)

NOVELIST

Hawthorne had already published his great novels, including *The Scarlet Letter* and *The House of the Seven Gables,* by the time he visited wartime Washington in 1862. There he met and "interviewed" President Lincoln—not in the sense that modern journalists interrogate politicians, but rather for a brief chat during a presentation ceremony in the White House. "I have shaken hands with Uncle Abe," Hawthorne wrote home proudly on March 16.

When Hawthorne returned to Massachusetts, the editor of the *Atlantic Monthly* invited him to submit a piece about his trip. The magazine was horrified by Hawthorne's candid description of the President and insisted he change it; Hawthorne refused, instead deleting the entire section and inserting an "editorial note" suggesting that the "personal" observation had been deleted because "it lacks relevance." "I really think you omit the only part of the article really worth publishing," he confided to his editor. "Upon my honor, it seems to me to have a historical value—but let it go." His priceless description of his visit with Lincoln, resurrected, uncensored, after more than a century and a quarter, is among the most unforgettable ever written. ✢

NINE O'CLOCK HAD BEEN APPOINTED AS THE TIME FOR RECEIVING THE DEPUTATION, AND WE WERE PUNCTUAL TO THE MOMENT; BUT NOT SO THE PRESIDENT, WHO SENT US WORD that he was eating his breakfast, and would come as soon as he could. His appetite, we were glad to think, must have been a pretty fair one; for we waited about half an hour in one of the antechambers, and then we were ushered into a reception room, in one corner of which sat the Secretaries of War and of the Treasury, expecting, like ourselves, the termination of the Presidential breakfast. During this interval there were several new additions to our group, one or two of whom were in a working-garb, so that we formed a very miscellaneous collection of people, mostly unknown to each other, and without any common sponsor, but all with an equal right to look our head-servant in the face.

By and by there was a little stir on the staircase and in the passageway, and in lounged a tall, loose-jointed figure, of an exaggerated Yankee port and demeanor, whom (as being about the homeliest man I ever saw, yet by no means repulsive or disagreeable) it was impossible not to recognize as Uncle Abe.

Unquestionably, Western man though he be, and Kentuckian by birth, President Lincoln is the essential representative of all Yankees, and the veritable specimen, physically, of what the world seems determined to regard as our characteristic qualities. It is the strangest and yet the fittest thing in the jumble of human vicissitudes, that he, out of so many millions, unlooked for, unselected by any intelligible process that could be based upon his genuine qualities, unknown to those who chose him, and unsuspected of what endowments may adapt him for his tremendous responsibility, should have found the way open for him to fling his lank personality into the chair of state— where, I presume, it was his first impulse to throw his legs on the council-table, and tell the Cabinet Ministers a story.

There is no describing his lengthy awkwardness, nor the uncouthness of his movement; and yet it seemed as if I had been in the habit of seeing him daily, and had shaken hands with him a thousand times in some village street; so true was he to the aspect of the pattern American, though with a certain extravagance which, possibly, I exaggerated still further by the delighted eagerness with which I took it in. If put to guess his calling and livelihood, I should have taken him for a country schoolmaster as soon as anything else.

He was dressed in a rusty black frock-coat and pantaloons, unbrushed, and worn so faithfully that the suit had adapted itself to the curves and angularities of his figure, and had grown to be an outer skin of the man. He had shabby slippers on his feet. His hair was black, still unmixed with gray, stiff, somewhat bushy, and had apparently been acquainted with neither brush nor comb that morning, after the disarrangement of the pillow; and as to a nightcap, Uncle Abe probably knows nothing of such effeminacies. His complexion is dark and sallow, betokening, I fear, an insalubrious atmosphere around the White House; he has thick black eyebrows and an impending brow; his nose is large, and the lines about his mouth are very strongly defined.

The whole physiognomy is as coarse a one as you would meet anywhere in the length and breadth of the States; but, withal, it is redeemed, illuminated, softened, and brightened by a kindly though serious look out of his eyes, and an expression of homely sagacity, that seems weighted with rich results of village experience.

A great deal of native sense; no bookish cultivation, no refinement; honest at heart, and thoroughly so, and yet, in some sort, sly— at least, endowed with a sort of tact and wisdom that are akin to craft, and would impel him, I think, to take an antagonist in flank, rather than to make a bull-run at him right in front. But, on the whole, I like this sallow, queer, sagacious visage, with the homely human sympathies that warmed it; and, for my small share in the matter, would as lief have Uncle Abe for a ruler as any man whom it would have been practicable to put in his place.

Immediately on his entrance the President accosted our member of Congress, who had us in charge, and, with a comical twist of his face, made some jocular remark about the length of his breakfast. He then greeted us all round, not waiting for an introduction, but shaking and squeezing everybody's hand with the utmost cordiality, whether the individual's name was announced to him or not. His manner towards us was wholly without pretence, but yet had a kind of natural dignity, quite sufficient to keep the forwardest of us from clapping him on the shoulder and asking him for a story. A mutual acquaintance being established, our leader took the whip [a gift for Lincoln—ed.] out of its case, and began to read the address of presentation. The whip was an exceedingly long one, its handle wrought in ivory (by some artist in the Massachusetts State Prison, I believe), and ornamented with a medallion of the President, and other equally beautiful devices; and along its whole length there was a succession of gold bands and ferrules. The address was shorter than the whip, but equally well made, consisting chiefly of an explanatory description of these artistic designs, and closing with a hint that the gift was a suggestive and emblematic one, and that the President would recognize the use to which such an instrument should be put.

This suggestion gave Uncle Abe rather a delicate task in his reply, because, slight as the matter seemed, it apparently called for some declaration, or intimation, or faint foreshadowing of policy in reference to the conduct of the war, and the final treatment of the Rebels. But the President's Yankee aptness and not-to-be-caughtness stood him in good stead, and he jerked or wiggled himself out of the dilemma with an uncouth dexterity that was entirely in character; although, without his jesticulation [*sic*] of eye and mouth—and especially the flourish of the whip, with which he imagined himself touching up a pair of fat horses—I doubt whether his words would be worth recording, even if I could remember them. The gist of the reply was, that he accepted the whip as an emblem of peace, not punishment; and, this great affair over, we retired out of the presence in high good-humor, only regretting that we could not have seen the President sit down and fold up his legs (which is said to be a most extraordinary spectacle), or have

heard him tell one of those delectable stories for which he is so celebrated. A good many of them are afloat upon the common talk of
Washington, and are certainly the aptest, pithiest, and funniest little
things imaginable; though, to be sure, they smack of the frontier freedom, and would not always bear repetition in a drawing-room, or on
the immaculate page of the *Atlantic*.

Good Heavens! what liberties have I been taking with one of the
potentates of the earth, and the man on whose conduct more important consequences depend than on that of any other historical personage of the century! But with whom is an American citizen entitled
to take a liberty, if not with his own chief magistrate? However, lest
the above allusions to President Lincoln's little peculiarities (already
well known to the country and to the world) should be misinterpreted, I deem it proper to say a word or two in regard to him, of un-
feigned respect and measurable confidence. He is evidently a man of
keen faculties, and, what is still more to the purpose, of powerful character. As to his integrity, the people have that intuition of it which is
never deceived. Before he actually entered upon his great office, and
for a considerable time afterwards, there is no reason to suppose that
he adequately estimated the gigantic task about to be imposed [on]
him, or, at least, had any distinct idea how it was to be managed; and
I presume there may have been more than one veteran politician who
proposed himself to take the power out of President Lincoln's hands
into his own, leaving our honest friend only the public responsibility
for the good or ill success of the career. The extremely imperfect de-

velopment of his statesmanly qualities, at that period, may have justified such designs. But the President is teachable by events, and has now spent a year in a very arduous course of education; he has a flexible mind, capable of much expansion, and convertible towards far loftier studies and activities than those of his early life; and if he came to Washington a backwoods humorist, he has already transformed himself into as good a statesman (to speak moderately) as his prime-minister [a reference to Secretary of State William H. Seward—ed.].

"One Raised Through the Commonest Average of Life"

WALT WHITMAN
(1819–1892)
POET

During the Civil War Whitman's brother George was wounded in action, and the poet, who had already published *Leaves of Grass,* rushed to Virginia to nurse him back to health. After George's recovery, the poet went to Washington to volunteer as a nurse in military hospitals, serving, as a nineteenth-century biographical sketch put it, "as care-taker for the worst cases of sick and wounded of both armies." It was in the capital that Whitman first glimpsed—and was profoundly affected by—Abraham Lincoln. Although he never developed a speaking relationship with the President, Whitman soon came to regard the tall, sad figure almost as a friend.

Whitman went on to write recollections of wartime Washington in *Drum Taps,* later editions of which featured his great elegy to Lincoln, "When Lilacs Last in the Dooryard Bloom'd." The poet would become indelibly associated with Lincoln with the appearance of his rather uncharacteristically conventional—and hugely popular—verse "O Captain! My Captain."

The comments that follow come from Whitman's collection *Specimen Days,* which also drew on his wartime journals; and from the 1888 volume, *Reminiscences of Abraham Lincoln by Distinguished Men of His Time.* ❖

———◆———

FROM MY NOTE-BOOK IN 1864, AT WASHINGTON CITY, I FIND THIS MEMORANDUM, UNDER DATE OF AUGUST 12: I SEE THE PRESIDENT ALMOST EVERY DAY, AS I HAPPEN TO LIVE WHERE HE passes to or from his lodgings out of town. He never sleeps at the White House during the hot season, but has quarters at a healthy location, some three miles north of the city, the Soldiers' Home, a United States military establishment. I saw him this morning about 8½ coming in to business, riding on Vermont Avenue, near L street. The sight is a significant one, (and different enough from how and where I first saw him).

(I shall not easily forget the first time I saw Abraham Lincoln. It must have been about the 18th or 19th of February, 1861. It was rather a pleasant spring afternoon, in New York City, as Lincoln arrived there from the West to stop a few hours and then pass on to Washington, to prepare for his inauguration. I saw him in Broadway, near the site of the present Post-office. He had come down, I think, from Canal street, to stop at the Astor House. The broad spaces, sidewalks, and street in the neighborhood, and for some distance, were crowded with solid masses of people, many thousands. The omnibuses and other vehicles had been all turn'd off, leaving an unusual hush in that busy part of the city. Presently two or three shabby hack barouches made their way with some difficulty through the crowd, and drew up at the Astor House entrance. A tall figure step'd out of the centre of these barouches, paus'd leisurely on the sidewalk, look'd up at the dark granite walls and looming architecture of the grand old hotel—then, after a relieving stretch of arms and legs, turn'd round for over a minute to slowly and good-humoredly scan the appearance of the vast and silent crowds—and so, with very moderate pace, and accompanied by a few unknown-looking persons, ascended the portico steps.

The figure, the look, the gait, are distinctly impress'd upon me yet; the unusual and uncouth height, the dress of complete black, the stovepipe hat push'd back on the head, the dark-brown complexion, the seam'd and wrinkled yet canny-looking face, the black, bushy head of hair, the disproportionately long neck, and the hands held behind as he stood observing the people. All was comparative and ominous silence. The new comer look'd with curiosity upon that immense sea of faces, and the sea of faces return'd the look with similar curiosity. In both there was a dash of something almost comical. Yet there was much anxiety in certain quarters. Cautious persons had fear'd that there would be some outbreak, some mark'd indignity or insult to the President elect on his passage through the city, for he possess'd no personal popularity in New York, and not much political. No such outbreak or insult, however, occurr'd. Only the silence of the crowd was very significant to those who were accustom'd to the usual demonstrations of New York in wild, tumultuous hurrahs—the deafening tumults of welcome, and the thunder-shouts of pack'd myriads along the whole line of Broadway, receiving Hungarian Kossuth or Filibuster Walker.)

He always has a company of twenty-five or thirty cavalry, with sabres drawn, and held upright over their shoulders. The party makes no great show in uniforms or horses. Mr. Lincoln, on the saddle, generally rides a good-sized easy-going gray horse, is dress'd in plain black, somewhat rusty and dusty; wears a black stiff hat, and looks about as ordinary in attire, &c., as the commonest man. A Lieutenant, with yellow straps, rides at his left, and following behind, two by two, come the cavalry men in their yellow-striped jackets. They are generally going at a slow trot, as that is the pace set them by the One they wait upon. The sabres and accoutrements clank, and the entirely unornamental *cortege* as it trots towards Lafayette square, arouses no sensation, only some curious stranger stops and gazes. I see very plainly ABRAHAM

LINCOLN'S dark brown face, with the deep cut lines, the eyes, &c., always to me with a deep latent sadness in the expression. We have got so that we always exchange bows, and very cordial ones.

Abraham Lincoln's was really one of those characters, the best of which is the result of long trains of cause and effect—needing a certain spaciousness of time, and perhaps even remoteness, to properly enclose them—having unequaled influence on the shaping of this Republic (and therefore the world) as to-day, and then far more important in the future. Thus the time has by no means yet come for a thorough measurement of him. Nevertheless, we who live in his era—who have seen him, and heard him, face to face, and are in the midst of, or just parting from, the strong and strange events which he and we have had to do with, can in some respects bear valuable, perhaps indispensable testimony concerning him. . . .

How does this man compare with the acknowledged "Father of his country?" Washington was modeled on the best Saxon and Franklin of the age of the Stuarts (rooted in the Elizabethan period)—was essentially a noble Englishman, and just the kind needed for the occasions and the times of 1776–'83. Lincoln, underneath his practicality, was far less European, far more Western, original, essentially non-conventional, and had a certain sort of out-door or prairie stamp. One of the best of the late commentators on Shakespeare (Professor Dowden), makes the height and aggregate of his quality as a poet to be, that he thoroughly blended the ideal with the practical or realistic. If this be so, I should say that what Shakespeare did in poetic expression, Abraham Lincoln essentially did in his personal and official life. I should say the invisible foundations and vertebra of his character, more than any man's history, were mystical, abstract, moral and spiritual—while upon all of them was built, and out of all of them radiated, under the control of the average of circumstances, what the vulgar call *horse-sense,* and a life often bent by temporary but most urgent materialistic and political reasons. . . .

I have fancied, I say, some such venerable relic of this time of ours, preserved to the next or still the next generation of America. I have fancied on such occasion, the young men gathering around; the awe, the eager questions. "What! Have you seen Abraham Lincoln— and heard him speak—and touched his hand? Have you, with your own eyes, looked on Grant, and Lee and Sherman?"

Dear to Democracy, to the very last! And among the paradoxes generated by America not the least curious, was that spectacle of all the kings and queens and emperors of the earth, many from remote distances, sending tributes of condolence and sorrow in memory of one raised through the commonest average of life—a rail-splitter and flat-boatman!

Considered from contemporary points of view—who knows what the future may decide?—and from the points of view of current Democracy and The Union (the only thing like passion or infatuation in the man was the passion for the Union of These States), Abraham Lincoln seems to me the grandest figure yet, on all the crowded canvas of the Nineteenth Century.

"The Best Abused Man of Our Nation"

HARRIET BEECHER STOWE

(1811–1896)

AUTHOR

By the time the celebrated Mrs. Stowe met Lincoln in the White House in November 1862, slavery, the institution she opposed so passionately, had finally been dealt its death blow by the President's preliminary Emancipation Proclamation. Stowe had aroused the nation with her 1852 novel, *Uncle Tom's Cabin, or Life among the Lowly.* It became a huge best seller and, some historians believe, hastened the secession crisis. According to legend, when Lincoln was at last introduced to the author, he exclaimed: "Is this the little woman who made this great war?"

Stowe did not immediately publish an account of her interview with Lincoln, but an article did appear contemporaneously, in the 6 February 1864 issue of a periodical called *Littell's Living Age,* from which the following observations are excerpted. ✥

LINCOLN IS A STRONG MAN, BUT HIS STRENGTH IS OF A PECU-
LIAR KIND; IT IS NOT AGGRESSIVE SO MUCH AS PASSIVE, AND
AMONG PASSIVE THINGS, IT IS LIKE THE STRENGTH NOT SO
much of a stone buttress as of a wire cable. It is strength swaying to
every influence, yielding on this side and on that to popular needs, yet
tenaciously, inflexibly bound to carry its great end; and probably by
no other kind of strength could our national ship have been drawn
safely thus far during the tossings and tempests which beset her way.

Surrounded by all sorts of conflicting claims, by traitors, by half-
hearted, timid men, by Border States men, and Free States men, by
radical Abolitionists and Conservatives, he has listened to all, weighed
the words of all, waited, observed, yielded now here and now there,
but in the main kept one inflexible, honest purpose, and drawn the national ship through.

In times of our trouble Abraham Lincoln has had his turn of
being the best abused man of our nation. Like Moses leading his Israel
through the wilderness, he has seen the day when every man seemed
ready to stone him, and yet, with simple, wiry, steady perseverance, he
has held on, conscious of honest intentions and looking to God for
help. All the nation have felt, in the increasing solemnity of his procla-
mations and papers, how deep an education was being wrought in his
mind by this simple faith in God, the ruler of nations, and this humble willingness to learn the awful lessons of his providence.

We do not mean to give the impression that Lincoln is a religious man in the sense in which that term is popularly applied. We believe he has never made any such profession, but we see evidence that in passing through this dreadful national crisis he has been forced by the very anguish of the struggle to look upward, where any rational creature must look for support. No man in this agony has suffered more and deeper, albeit with a dry, weary, patient pain, that seemed to some like insensibility. "Whichever way it ends," he said to the writer, "I have the impression that *I* sha'n't last long after it's over." After the dreadful repulse of Fredericksburg, his heavy eyes and worn and weary air told how our reverses wore upon him, and yet there was a never-failing fund of patience at bottom that sometimes rose to the surface in some droll, quaint saying, or story, that forced a laugh even from himself.

There have been times with many, of impetuous impatience, when our national ship seemed to lie water-logged and we have called aloud for a deliverer of another fashion—a brilliant general, a dashing, fearless statesman, a man who could dare and do, and who would stake all on a die, and win or lose by a brilliant *coup de main*. It may comfort our minds that since He who ruleth in the armies of nations set no such man to this work, that perhaps He saw in the man whom He did send some peculiar fitness and aptitudes therefor.

Slow and careful in coming to resolutions, willing to talk with every person who has anything to show on any side of a disputed subject, long in weighing and pondering, attached to constitutional limits and time-honored landmarks, Lincoln certainly was the *safest* leader a nation could have at a time when the *habeas corpus* must be suspended, and all the constitutional and minor rights of citizens be thrown into the hands of their military leader. A reckless, bold, theorizing, dashing man of genius might have wrecked our Constitution and ended us in a splendid military despotism.

Among the many accusations which in hours of ill-luck have been thrown out upon Lincoln, it is remarkable that he has never been called self-seeking, or selfish. When we were troubled and sat in darkness, and looked doubtfully towards the presidential chair, it was never that we doubted the goodwill of our pilot—only the clearness of his eyesight. But Almighty God has granted to him that clearness of vision which he gives to the true-hearted, and enabled him to set his honest foot in that promised land of freedom which is to be the patrimony of all men, black and white—and from henceforth nations shall rise up to call him blessed.

9. MEMORIES FROM ARTISTS

I t is one of the ironies of American history that Lincoln—whose physical appearance was ridiculed by opponents and often denigrated by the sixteenth president himself—became one of the most popular and important subjects for the portrait painters and sculptors of his era.

For the last five years of his life, Lincoln posed frequently for artists who worked in several media, allowing them to make sketches and take measurements while he worked, and bantering with them as they tried to capture his elusive features. For a man supposedly unenlightened about the importance of image in history, Lincoln was remarkably sensitive to requests for the time and patience required to record that image. At one point, for six months, he even had what might be called a "court artist" working in the White House on a historical canvas celebrating the Emancipation Proclamation. Lincoln called himself an "indifferent judge" of his own pictures. But he was wise enough to make sure that they got made.

Artists who later wrote reminiscences about their sittings with Lincoln agreed about one thing: that he was the most challenging subject they ever painted or sculpted. Such self-serving recollections made them seem greater craftsmen, of course, but there is evidence that there was some truth to their observations. When animated, Lincoln's features were mobile and expressive. But sitting rigidly for artists, he typically lapsed into a dreamy trance. "This was not he who smiled, spoke, laughed, charmed," his private secretary lamented about one likeness, agreeing that "Lincoln's features were the despair of every artist who undertook his portrait."

The artists represented in this section include Leonard Wells Volk, who took a life mask of Lincoln before the Illinois politician became famous; Thomas D. Jones, who made a sculpture during the days Lincoln prepared to assume the presidency; and Francis B. Carpenter, the "court artist" who came to know his subject so well that he wrote an entire memoir about his experiences, entitling its second edition *The Inner Life of Abraham Lincoln*. Today, Lincoln's fatherly, bearded image is one of America's most familiar. It was not always so well known. These are the recollections of the men who made it famous. ✤

"The Animal Himself"

LEONARD WELLS VOLK

(1828–1895)

SCULPTOR

Volk was a cousin by marriage of Lincoln's lifelong political rival, Stephen A. Douglas. After studies in Rome, he returned to America, opened a studio in Chicago, and produced an acclaimed statue of his famous relative. During Douglas's celebrated debates with Abraham Lincoln in 1858, the Republican challenger came to the sculptor's attention. Political and family affiliations notwithstanding, Volk determined to portray Lincoln, too. The decision ensured Volk's fame and fortune.

In 1860 Volk made a plaster cast of Lincoln's face and hands, from which he modeled two public statues and a number of smaller busts that were mass-produced in plaster and bronze. Judging by the number of copies that survive, the busts were highly popular and carefully preserved. Sixteen years after the assassination, Volk wrote a charming reminiscence about his encounters with Lincoln—one of the best such accounts ever written by an artist. An excerpt follows. ✛

H E ENTERED MY STUDIO ON SUNDAY MORNING, REMARKING THAT A FRIEND AT THE HOTEL (TREMONT HOUSE) HAD IN- VITED HIM TO ATTEND CHURCH, "BUT," SAID MR. LINCOLN, "I thought I'd rather come and sit for the bust. The fact is," he continued, "I don't like to hear cut and dried sermons. No—when I hear a man preach, I like to see him act as if he were fighting bees!" And he ex- tended his long arms, at the same time suiting the action to the words. He gave me on this day a sitting of more than four hours, and when it was concluded, went to our family apartment, on the corner of the building across the corridor from the studio, to look at a collection of photographs which I had made in 1855–6–7, in Rome and Florence. While sitting in the rocking-chair, he took my little son on his lap and spoke kindly to him, asking his name, age, etc. I held the photographs up and explained them to him, but I noticed a growing weariness, and his eyelids closed occasionally as if he were sleepy, or were thinking of something besides Grecian and Roman statuary and architecture. Fi- nally he said: "These things must be very interesting to you, Mr. Volk, but the truth is I don't know much of history, and all I do know of it I have learned from lawbooks."

The sittings were continued daily till the Thursday following, and, during their continuance, he would talk almost unceasingly, telling some of the funniest and most laughable of stories, but he talked little of politics or religion during those sittings. He said: "I am bored nearly every time I sit down to a public dining-table by some one pitching into me on politics." Upon one occasion he spoke most enthusiastically of his profound admiration of Henry Clay, saying that he "almost worshiped him."

I remember, also, that he paid a high compliment to the late William A. Richardson, and said: "I regard him as one of the truest men that ever lived; he sticks to Judge Douglas through thick and thin—never deserted him, and never will. I admire such a man! By the by, Mr. Volk, he is now in town, and stopping at the Tremont. May I bring him with me tomorrow to see the bust?" Accordingly, he brought him and two other old friends, ex-Lieut.-Gov. McMurtry, of Illinois, and Ebenezer Peck, all of whom looked a moment at the clay model, saying it was "just like him!" Then they began to tell stories and rehearse reminiscences, one after another. I can imagine I now hear their hearty laughs, just as I can see, as if photographed, the tall figure of Lincoln striding across that stubble-field.

Many people, presumably political aspirants with an eye to future prospects, besieged my door for interviews, but I made it a rule to keep it locked, and I think Mr. Lincoln appreciated the precaution.

The last sitting was given Thursday morning, and I noticed that Mr. Lincoln was in something of a hurry. I had finished the head, but desired to represent his breast and brawny shoulders as nature presented them; so he stripped off his coat, waistcoat, shirt, cravat, and collar, threw them on a chair, pulled his undershirt down a short distance, tying the sleeves behind him, and stood up without a murmur for an hour or so. I then said that I was done, and was a thousand times obliged to him for his promptness and patience, and offered to assist him to re-dress, but he said: "No, I can do it better alone." I kept at my work without looking toward him, wishing to catch the form as accurately as possible while it was fresh in my memory. Mr. Lincoln left hurriedly, saying he had an engagement, and with a cordial "Good-bye! I will see you again soon," passed out. A few moments after, I recognized his steps rapidly returning. The door opened, and in he came, exclaiming: "Hello, Mr. Volk! I got down on the sidewalk and found I had forgotten to put on my undershirt, and thought it wouldn't do to go through the streets this way." Sure enough, there were the sleeves of that garment dangling below the skirts of his broadcloth frock coat! I went at once to his assistance, and helped to undress and re-dress him all right, and out he went, with a hearty laugh at the absurdity of the thing.

On a Thursday in the month of June [it was actually May—ed.] following, Mr. Lincoln received the nomination on the third ballot for President of the United States. And it happened that on the same day I was on the cars, nearing Springfield. About midday, we reached Bloomington, and there learned of his nomination. At three or four o'clock, we arrived at our destination. The afternoon was lovely— bright and sunny, neither too warm nor too cool; the grass, trees, and the hosts of blooming roses, so profuse in Springfield, appeared to be vying with the ringing bells and waving flags.

As soon as I had brushed off the dust and registered at the old Chenery House, I went straight to Mr. Lincoln's unpretentious little two-story house. He saw me from his door or window coming down the street, and as I entered the gate, he was on the platform in front of the door, and quite alone. His face looked radiant. I exclaimed: "I am the first man from Chicago, I believe, who has the honor of congratulating you on your nomination for President." Then those two great hands took both of mine with a grasp never to be forgotten. And while shaking, I said: "Now that you will doubtless be the next President of the United States, I want to make a statue of you, and shall do my best to do you justice." Said he, "I don't doubt it, for I have come to the conclusion that you are an honest man," and with that greeting I thought my hands were in a fair way of being crushed. I was invited into the parlor, and soon Mrs. Lincoln entered, holding a rose bouquet in her hand, which she presented to me after the introduction; and in return I gave her a cabinet-size bust of her husband, which I had modeled from the large one, and happened to have with me. Before leaving the house, it was arranged that Mr. Lincoln would give Saturday forenoon to obtaining full-length photographs to serve me for the proposed statue. . . .

The last time I saw Mr. Lincoln was in January, 1861, at his house in Springfield. His little parlor was full of friends and politicians. He introduced me to them all, and remarked to me aside that, since he had sat for me for his bust, he had lost forty pounds in weight. This was easily perceptible, for the lines of his jaws were very sharply defined through the short beard which he was allowing to grow. Then he returned to the company, and announced in a general way that I had made a bust of him before his nomination, and that he was then giving daily sittings, at the St. Nicholas Hotel, to another sculptor [Thomas D. Jones—ed.]; that he had sat to him for a week or more, but could not see the likeness, though he might yet bring it out.

"But," continued Mr. Lincoln, "in two or three days after Mr. Volk commenced my bust, there was the animal himself!"

"There Are Few Such Men in the World"

THOMAS D. JONES
(1811–1881)
SCULPTOR

A native of upstate New York, Jones began his career as a stonemason, then moved to Cincinnati, building a reputation as a sculptor, and attracting such prominent sitters as Henry Clay and Zachary Taylor. Following Lincoln's election in November 1860, Jones was commissioned to make a portrait bust from life of the president-elect. He arrived in Springfield on Christmas and the next day introduced himself to his subject at Lincoln's temporary office at the Illinois State Capitol. There, Jones explained his method to a visibly relieved Lincoln, who remembered as "anything but agreeable" the recent experience of having a wet-plaster cast made of his face. Lincoln sat for the artist daily in his hotel room. There, Jones modeled him as Lincoln read his mail.

Jones, who created a second life bust of Lincoln in 1864, published a detailed recollection of his initial experience with his famous sitter in the *Sacramento Union* on 4 November 1871. It offered a revealing glimpse of the newly elected President on the eve of his inauguration—waiting patiently but powerlessly to assume office while the storm of the secession crisis gathered fearsome momentum around him. ✥

———✥———

T HE WORK ONCE BEGUN, HE BECAME A SUBJECT OF GREAT IN-TEREST, BUT A VERY DIFFICULT STUDY. HIS EARLY MODE OF LIFE AND HABITS OF THOUGHT HAD IMPRESSED HARD AND rugged lines upon his face, but a good anecdote or story before com-mencing a sitting much improved the plastic character of his features.

He received letters almost daily from the South on all sorts of subjects—some coarse, some witty, and others amusing. The most fre-quent inquiries of him were those on the subject of rail splitting—the best timber for rails, which end to split first—buttered or top end, all of which never disturbed the equanimity of his temper. . . .

About two weeks before Lincoln left Springfield for Washington a deep-seated melancholy seemed to take possession of his soul. While James Buchanan, sitting like Cerberus at the gate, would neither do, nor let others act, South Carolina had already seceded, and other States [were] preparing to do the same damnable deed. The great problem with Lincoln at the time was, How to enforce the laws in the true spirit of the Constitution without the shedding of blood. During those two weeks he made not a single threat, apparently resigned to his fate, as a martyr prepared for the stake. The former Lincoln was no longer visible to me. His face was transformed from mobility into an iron mask. . . .

Lincoln's keen perception of the ridiculous enabled him to enjoy an anecdote or story better than most men, and he treasured them too. While in a photograph gallery one morning, posing him for some pictures he desired to present a very dear friend, I tried to recall two lines of A. J. H. Duganne's "Parnassus in Pillory," written by him twenty years ago. All I could remember ran as follows:

> Endymion Hurst, whose head,
> Unlike his books, is red.

They pleased him better than I anticipated, and I rehearsed them several times until they were fixed in his memory.

We generally opened the ball in the morning with two or three anecdotes, each, and then went on with our work in silence. Should a story or anecdote not be clearly impressed upon his mind the next day he would ask me to repeat it. He had a remarkable memory of events, of language, of persons and things, but not of names. Desiring to illustrate something, one day, by telling an anecdote, to Judge Swain, he said: "Judge, what is that man's name in Ohio that makes mud heads?" "Jones." "You are right, that reminds me of one of his stories. . . ."

. . . His head was neither Greek nor Roman, nor Celt, for his upper lip was too short for that, or a Low German. There are few such men in the world. Where they came from originally is not positively known. The profile line of the forehead and nose resembled each other.

General Jackson was one of that type of men. They have no depression in their forehead at that point called eventuality. The line of the forehead from the root of the nose to the hair above comparison is slightly convex. Such men remember everything and forget nothing. Their eyes are not large, hence their deliberation of speech; neither are they bon vivants or bald-headed.

Lincoln was decidedly one of that class of men. His habit of thought and a very delicate digestion gave him a lean face and a spare figure. He had a fine head of hair until the barbers at Washington attended to his toilette. Twelve men out of thirteen wear their hair parted on the left side of the heads—why? Because nearly all our barbers use their right hand in their profession instead of their left.

Before the public Lincoln was a very grave and earnest man; in private, kind, modest, and replete with wit and humor. He never told a story for its zanyism, but purely for good humor, illustration, or "adornment of his speech," as Rabelais would say. As an evidence of Lincoln's kindly nature in domestic life, an old milkman called to see his bust. He said he had served Lincoln with milk for several years; that Lincoln would walk over to his place in the morning barefooted with a little bucket in one hand, and his oldest boy sitting astride of his shoulders, chirping like a bird.

"Mr. Lincoln Had the Saddest Face"

FRANCIS BICKNELL CARPENTER

(1830–1900)

ARTIST

What he lacked in painterly skill, Carpenter balanced with political zeal and a keen eye for marketable images. An ardent anti-slavery Republican from upstate New York, he greeted news of the Emancipation Proclamation by conceiving an ambitious plan to consecrate it in a major historical picture. Understanding that Lincoln's act was "second only in historical importance . . . to the Declaration of Independence," Carpenter armed himself with introductions from influential congressmen and traveled to Washington. There Lincoln agreed to sit for him and granted him permission to use the White House as a studio while he worked on his canvas.

The artist spent nearly six months at the task, and the result was *The First Reading of the Emancipation Proclamation of President Lincoln,* a monumental picture that won much critical acclaim. It was exhibited on a national tour, and eventually purchased for the government and presented in 1878 to the U.S. Capitol, where it still hangs. But its reputation had been secured years earlier through a hugely successful engraved adaptation published in 1866.

That same year, Carpenter brought out a book about his experiences in the Executive Mansion. It prompted Mary Lincoln to denounce him as one of those "silly adventurers with whom my husband had scarcely the least acquaintance," but the public believed Carpenter. His volume went into several editions and has remained a principal source of anecdotes about Lincoln's White House routine.

Earlier, Carpenter wrote a largely forgotten afterword to Henry J. Raymond's 1865 biography, *The Life and Public Services of Abraham Lincoln,* not coincidentally published by the same firm that issued the engraving of Carpenter's painting. It is from that piece, "Anecdotes and Reminiscences of President Lincoln," that the first of the following excerpts is drawn—the early recollections of the man who virtually became Lincoln's artist-in-residence. The second reminiscence, which comes from Carpenter's own book, *Six Months at the White House,* suggests that even the famously patient Lincoln could occasionally be driven over the edge by audacious favor-seekers. ✢

IT HAS BEEN THE BUSINESS OF MY LIFE TO STUDY THE HUMAN FACE, AND I HAVE SAID REPEATEDLY TO FRIENDS THAT MR. LINCOLN HAD THE SADDEST FACE I EVER ATTEMPTED TO PAINT. During some of the dark days of the spring and summer of 1864, I saw him at times when his care-worn, troubled appearance was enough to bring tears of sympathy into the eyes of his most bitter opponents. I recall particularly one day, when, having occasion to pass through the main hall of the domestic apartments, I met him alone, pacing up and down a narrow passage, his hands behind him, his head bent forward upon his breast, heavy black rings under his eyes, showing sleepless nights—altogether such a picture of the effects of sorrow and care as I have never seen! . . .

Mr. Lincoln could scarcely be called a *religious* man, in the common acceptation of the term, and yet a sincerer *Christian* I believe never lived. A constitutional tendency to dwell upon sacred things; an emotional nature which finds ready expression in religious conversation and revival meetings; the culture and development of the devotional element till the expression of religious thought and experience becomes almost habitual, were not among his characteristics. Doubtless he felt as deeply upon the great questions of the soul and eternity as any other thoughtful man, but the very tenderness and humility of his nature would not permit the exposure of his inmost convictions, except upon the rarest occasions, and to his most intimate friends. And yet, aside from emotional expression, I believe no man had a more abiding sense of his dependence upon God, or faith in the Divine government, and in the power and ultimate triumph of Truth and Right in the world.

A great deal has been said of the uniform meekness and kindness of heart of Mr. Lincoln, but there would sometimes be afforded evidence that one grain of sand too much would break even *this* camel's back. Among the callers at the White House one day, was an officer who had been cashiered from the service. He had prepared an elaborate defense of himself, which he consumed much time in reading to the President. When he had finished, Mr. Lincoln replied that even upon his own statement of the case, the facts would not warrant executive interference.

Disappointed, and considerably crestfallen, the man withdrew. A few days afterward, he made a second attempt to alter the President's convictions, going over substantially the same ground, and occupying about the same space of time, but without accomplishing his end. The *third* time he succeeded in forcing himself into Mr. Lincoln's presence, who with great forbearance listened to another repetition of the case to its conclusion, but made no reply. Waiting for a moment, the man gathered from the expression of his countenance that his mind was unconvinced. Turning very abruptly, he said: "Well, Mr. President, I see you are fully determined not to do me justice!" This was too aggravating, even for Mr. Lincoln. Manifesting, however, no more feeling than that indicated by a slight compression of the lips, he very quietly arose, laid down a package of papers he held in his hand, and then suddenly seizing the defunct officer by the coat-collar, he marched him forcibly to the door, saying, as he ejected him into the passage: "Sir, I give you fair warning never to show yourself in this room again. I can bear censure, but not insult!" In a whining tone the man begged for his papers, which he had dropped. "Begone, sir," said the President, "your papers will be sent to you. I never wish to see your face again."

Upon another occasion, as I was going through the passage, the door of the President's office suddenly opened, and two ladies, one of whom seemed in a towering passion, were unceremoniously ushered out by one of the attendants. As they passed me on their way down the stairs, I overheard the elder remonstrating with her companion upon the violence of her expressions. I afterward asked old Daniel [one of the doormen—ed.] what had happened? "Oh," he replied, "the younger woman was very saucy to the President. She went one step too far; and he told me to show them out of the house."

10. MEMORIES FROM AFRICAN-AMERICANS

I t may at first glance seem politically incorrect to segregate into one discrete chapter the recollections of Lincoln by African-Americans. But in Lincoln's sphere, the races were separate and unequal. Black observers surely felt the weight of this rigid barrier in their dealings with the man who would become known as "the Great Emancipator." As historian John Hope Franklin has pointed out: "Lincoln could not have overcome the nation's strong prejudices toward racial separation if he had tried. And he did not try very hard."

Yet Lincoln counted among his greatest admirers the highly regarded missionary for tolerance, Sojourner Truth, and the most influential African-American leader of the century, Frederick Douglass. Both of them testified, in recollections of their meetings with the President, to his tolerance and hospitality. It is surely worth noting that these two visitors were the first African-Americans ever to enter the White House as guests, and both remembered him warmly.

Nor were Lincoln's meetings with Douglass merely ceremonial. In 1864 the two men together hatched a plan to recruit a civilian army to spread word of the year-old Emancipation Proclamation to slaves still held in bondage, and ignorance, in Confederate territory. Worried that he would be defeated for reelection by a Democrat eager to undo emancipation, Lincoln was determined to see as many slaves liberated before November as possible. Douglass later characterized the scheme as "evidence conclusive on Mr. Lincoln's part that the proclamation, so far at least as he was concerned, was not effected merely as a 'necessity,'" but as a sincere effort to end slavery forever.

The number of African-Americans who met Lincoln is small; the reminiscences included here represent the best examples. The president who began the process of freeing the slaves knew precious few African-Americans himself. And few African-Americans ever had the opportunity to know him. ✢

"In the Presence of a Friend"

SOJOURNER TRUTH
(1797–1883)
Ex-Slave, Evangelist

Born into slavery as Isabella Baumfree, Sojourner Truth became an abolitionist preacher in the 1840s, and by the dawn of the Civil War was the nation's best known African-American woman. She traveled throughout New England and the West, holding audiences spellbound with her deep voice and what historian John Hope Franklin has referred to as her "religious mysticism." Generations before Rosa Parks, she was also a freedom rider on Washington's segregated streetcars. And decades before the suffrage movement grew in influence, she was an advocate of women's rights.

On the morning of 29 October 1864, Sojourner Truth enjoyed her first and only meeting with the man she regarded as "the Emancipator of her race," according to a contemporary observer. Lincoln himself exhibited courage in welcoming a well-known black woman to the executive mansion only a week before election day.

Sojourner, who could not read or write, dictated her recollection of the meeting twice: to the woman who had accompanied her to the White House, and also in a letter transcribed by a friend. The following reminiscence is extrapolated from these two accounts, which are quite similar. ✣

I T WAS ABOUT EIGHT O'CLOCK A.M., WHEN I CALLED ON THE PRESIDENT. UPON ENTERING HIS RECEPTION-ROOM WE FOUND ABOUT A DOZEN PERSONS IN WAITING, AMONG THEM TWO COLORED women. I had quite a pleasant time waiting until he was disengaged, and enjoyed his conversation with others; he showed as much kindness and consideration to the colored persons as to the whites—if there was any difference, more. One case was that of a colored woman, who was sick and likely to be turned out of her house on account of her inability to pay her rent. The President listened to her with much attention, and spoke to her with kindness and tenderness.

He said he had given so much he could give no more, but told her where to go and get the money, and asked Mrs. [Lucy N.] C[olman]., who accompanied me, to assist her, which she did.

The President was seated at his desk. Mrs. C. said to him: "This is Sojourner Truth, who has come all the way from Michigan to see you." He then arose, gave me his hand, made a bow, and said: "I am pleased to see you."

I said to him: "Mr. President, when you first took your seat I feared you would be torn to pieces, for I likened you unto Daniel, who was thrown into the lions' den; and if the lions did not tear you into pieces, I knew that it would be God that had served you; and I said if He spared me I would see you before the four years expired, and He has done so, and now I am here to see you for myself."

He then congratulated me on my having been spared. Then I said: "I appreciate you, for you are the best President who has ever taken the seat." He replied thus: "I expect you have reference to my having emancipated the slaves in my proclamation. But," said he, mentioning the names of several of his predecessors (and among them emphatically that of Washington), "they were all just as good, and would have done just as I have done if the time had come. If the people over the river (pointing across the Potomac) had behaved themselves, I could not have done what I have; but they did not, and I was compelled to do ["had the opportunity to do" in the other version— ed.] these things." I then said: "I thank God that you were the instrument selected by Him and the people to do it."

He then showed me the Bible presented to him by the colored people of Baltimore, of which you have heard [received on September 7 and reported in the Washington *Star*—ed.]. I have seen it for myself, and it is beautiful beyond description. After I had looked it over, I said to him: "This is beautiful indeed; the colored people have given this to the Head of the Government, and that Government once sanctioned laws that would not permit its people to learn enough to enable them to read this Book. And for what? Let them answer who can."

I must say, and I am proud to say, that I never was treated by any one with more kindness and cordiality than was shown me by the great and good man, Abraham Lincoln, by the grace of God President of the United States for four years more. He took my little book, and with the same hand that signed the death-warrant of slavery, he wrote as follows:

For Aunty Sojourner Truth,
Oct. 29, 1864. A. Lincoln

As I was taking my leave, he arose and took my hand, and said he would be pleased to have me call again. I felt that I was in the presence of a friend, and I now thank God from the bottom of my heart that I always have advocated his cause, and have done it openly and boldly. I shall feel still more in duty bound to do so in time to come. May God assist me.

• • •

"Preeminently the White Man's President"

FREDERICK DOUGLASS

(1817–1895)

ABOLITIONIST

Born into slavery, Douglass escaped bondage and later purchased his own freedom, rising to become a leading abolitionist, an influential newspaper editor, and arguably the most important African-American leader of the nineteenth century. He was also the first prominent black man welcomed to the White House by Abraham Lincoln. Douglass visited the President on three separate occasions, remembering that Lincoln treated him professionally, and without condescension, extending him "a cordial hand, not too warm or too cold."

By the time the two men met, Douglass was nearly as famous as Lincoln. Although Douglass supported the Republican party, he and Lincoln did not always see eye to eye. For a time the abolitionist spokesman thought the President inexcusably slow on emancipation, although he led the applause from the black community when Lincoln issued his Emancipation Proclamation on 1 January 1863. Douglass later worked tirelessly to recruit black soldiers to fight to fulfill the promise of Lincoln's order.

Frederick Douglass's recollections of Lincoln are excerpted from two sources: his justly famous 1876 oration at the dedication of the Freedmen's monument in memory of Abraham Lincoln in 1876; and a chapter prepared for the 1888 collection, *Reminiscences of Abraham Lincoln by Distinguished Men of His Time*. ✤

O N MY APPROACH HE SLOWLY DREW HIS FEET IN FROM THE DIFFERENT PARTS OF THE ROOM INTO WHICH THEY HAD STRAYED, AND HE BEGAN TO RISE, AND CONTINUED TO RISE until he looked down upon me, and extended his hand and gave me a welcome. I began, with some hesitation, to tell him who I was and what I had been doing, but he soon stopped me, saying in a sharp, cordial voice:

"You need not tell me who you are, Mr. Douglass, I know who you are. Mr. [Samuel E.] Sewell [a longtime friend of Douglass's—ed.] has told me all about you."

He then invited me to take a seat beside him. Not wishing to occupy his time and attention, seeing that he was busy, I stated to him the object of my call at once. I said:

"Mr. Lincoln, I am recruiting colored troops. I have assisted in fitting up two regiments in Massachusetts, and am now at work in the same way in Pennsylvania, and have come to say this to you, sir, if you wish to make this branch of the service successful you must do four things:

"First—You must give colored soldiers the same pay that you give white soldiers.

"Second—You must compel the Confederate States to treat colored soldiers, when taken prisoners, as prisoners of war.

"Third—When any colored man or soldier performs brave, meritorious exploits in the field, you must enable me to say to those that I recruit that they will be promoted for such service, precisely as white men are promoted for similar service.

"Fourth—In case any colored soldiers are murdered in cold blood and taken prisoners, you should retaliate in kind."

To this little speech, Mr. Lincoln listened with earnest attention and with very apparent sympathy, and replied to each point in his own peculiar, forcible way. First he spoke of the opposition generally to employing negroes as soldiers at all, of the prejudice against the race, and of the advantage to colored people that would result from their being employed as soldiers in defense of their country. He regarded such an employment as an experiment, and spoke of the advantage it would be to the colored race if the experiment should succeed. He said that he had difficulty in getting colored men into the United States uniform; that when the purpose was fixed to employ them as soldiers, several different uniforms were proposed for them, and that it was something gained when it was finally determined to clothe them like other soldiers.

Now, as to the pay, we had to make some concession to prejudice. There were threats that if we made soldiers of them at all white men would not enlist, would not fight beside them. Besides, it was not believed that a negro could make a good soldier, as good a soldier as a white man, and hence it was thought that he should not have the same pay as a white man. But said he, "I assure you, Mr. Douglass, that in the end they shall have the same pay as white soldiers. . . ."

I met Mr. Lincoln several times after this interview.

I was once invited by him to take tea with him at the Soldiers' Home [Lincoln's summer residence outside Washington—ed.]. On one occasion, while visiting him at the White House, he showed me a letter he was writing to Horace Greeley [editor of the *New York Tribune*—ed.] in reply to some of Greeley's criticisms against protracting the war. He seemed to feel very keenly the reproaches heaped upon him for not bringing the war to a speedy conclusion; said he was charged with making it an Abolition war instead of a war for the Union, and expressed his desire to end the war as soon as possible. While I was talking with him Governor [William A.] Buckingham [of Connecticut—ed.] sent in his card, and I was amused by his telling the messenger, as well as by the way he expressed it, to "tell Governor Buckingham to wait, I want to have a long talk with my friend Douglass."

He used those words. I said: "Mr. Lincoln, I will retire." "Oh, no, no, you shall not, I want Governor Buckingham to wait," and he did wait for at least a half hour. When he came in I was introduced by Mr. Lincoln to Governor Buckingham, and the Governor did not seem to take it amiss at all that he had been required to wait.

I was present at the inauguration of Mr. Lincoln, the 4th of March, 1865. I felt then that there was murder in the air, and I kept close to his carriage on the way to the Capitol, for I felt that I might see him fall that day. It was a vague presentiment.

At that time the Confederate cause was on its last legs, as it were, and there was deep feeling. I could feel it in the atmosphere here. I did not know exactly what it was, but I just felt as if he might be shot on his way to the Capitol. I cannot refer to any incident, in fact, to any expression that I heard, it was simply a presentiment that Lincoln might fall that day. I got right in front of the east portico of the Capitol, listened to his inaugural address, and witnessed his being sworn in by Chief Justice Chase. When he came on the steps he was accompanied by Vice-President Johnson. In looking out in the crowd he saw me standing near by, and I could see he was pointing me out to Andrew Johnson. Mr. Johnson, without knowing perhaps that I saw the movement, looked quite annoyed that his attention should be called in that direction. So I got a peep into his soul. As soon as he saw me looking at him, suddenly he assumed rather an amicable expression of countenance. I felt that, whatever else the man might be, he was no friend to my people.

I heard Mr. Lincoln deliver this wonderful address. It was very short; but he answered all the objections raised to his prolonging the war in one sentence—it was a remarkable sentence.

"Fondly do we hope, profoundly do we pray, that this mighty scourge of war shall soon pass away, yet if God wills it continue until all the wealth piled up by two hundred years of bondage shall have been wasted, and each drop of blood drawn by the lash shall have been paid for by one drawn by the sword, we will still say, as was said three thousand years ago, the judgments of the Lord are true and righteous altogether."

For the first time in my life, and I suppose the first time in any colored man's life, I attended the reception of President Lincoln on the evening of the inauguration. As I approached the door I was seized by two policemen and forbidden to enter. I said to them that they were mistaken entirely in what they were doing, that if Mr. Lincoln knew that I was at the door he would order my admission, and I bolted in by them. On the inside I was taken charge of by two other policemen, to be conducted as I supposed to the President, but instead of that they were conducting me out the window on a plank.

"Oh," said I, "this will not do, gentlemen," and as a gentleman was passing in I said to him, "just say to Mr. Lincoln that Fred. Douglass is at the door."

He rushed in to President Lincoln, and almost in less than half a minute I was invited into the East Room of the White House. A perfect sea of beauty and elegance, too, it was. The ladies were in very fine attire, and Mrs. Lincoln was standing there. I could not have been more than ten feet from him when Mr. Lincoln saw me; his countenance lighted up, and he said in a voice which was heard all around: "Here comes my friend Douglass." As I approached him he reached out his hand, gave me a cordial shake, and said: "Douglass, I saw you in the crowd to-day listening to my inaugural address. There is no man's opinion that I value more than yours: what did you think of it?" I said: "Mr. Lincoln, I cannot stop here to talk with you, as there are thousands waiting to shake you by the hand;" but he said again: "What did you think of it?" I said: "Mr. Lincoln, it was a sacred effort," and then I walked off. "I am glad you liked it," he said. That was the last time I saw him to speak with him.

In all my interviews with Mr. Lincoln I was impressed with his entire freedom from popular prejudice against the colored race. He was the first great man that I talked with in the United States freely, who in no single instance reminded me of the difference between himself and myself, of the difference of color, and I thought that all the more remarkable because he came from a State where there were black laws. I account partially for his kindness to me because of the similarity with which I had fought my way up, we both starting at the lowest round of the ladder.

He was preeminently the white man's President, entirely devoted to the welfare of white men. He was ready and willing at any time during the first years of his administration to deny, postpone and sacrifice the rights of humanity in the colored people in order to promote the welfare of the white people of this country. In all his education and feeling he was an American of the Americans. He came into the presidential chair upon one principle alone, namely, opposition to the extension of slavery. His arguments in furtherance of this policy had their motive and mainspring in his patriotic devotion to the interests of his own race. To protect, defend, and perpetuate slavery in the States where it existed Abraham Lincoln was not less ready than any other president to draw the sword of the nation. He was ready to execute all the supposed constitutional guarantees of the United States Constitution in favor of the slave system anywhere inside the slave States. He was willing to pursue, recapture, and send back the fugitive slave to his master, and to suppress a slave rising for liberty, though the guilty master were already in arms against the Government. The race to which we belong were not the special objects of his consideration. . . .

I have said that President Lincoln was a white man and shared towards the colored race the prejudices common to his countrymen. Looking back to his times and to the conditions of his country, we are compelled to admit that this unfriendly feeling on his part may be safely set down as one element of his wonderful success in organizing the loyal American people for the tremendous conflict before them, and bringing them safely through that conflict. His great mission was to accomplish two things: first, to save his country from dismemberment and ruin; and second, to free his country from the great crime of slavery. To do one or the other, or both, he must have the earnest sympathy and the powerful cooperation of his loyal fellow-countrymen. Without this primary and essential condition to success his efforts must have been vain and utterly fruitless. Had he put the abolition of slavery before the salvation of the Union, he would have inevitably driven from him a powerful class of the American people and rendered assistance to rebellion impossible. Viewed from the genuine abolition ground, Mr. Lincoln seemed tardy, cold, dull, and indifferent; but measuring him by the sentiment of his country, a sentiment he was bound as a statesman to consult, he was swift, zealous, radical, and determined.

11. MEMORIES FROM WHITE HOUSE INTIMATES

Simplicity," a journalist of the day marveled, "was the main characteristic of Lincoln's White House."

Indeed, compared to the virtual army of employees serving modern presidents, the professional staff that worked in the Lincoln White House was minuscule. It consisted of just three private secretaries, one of whom was not even covered in the executive budget and had to be hired by a federal department and quietly "assigned" to Lincoln. Equally modest was the domestic staff.

The executive mansion of the Civil War era was primitive in other respects as well. Rebellion notwithstanding, it remained isolated from military communications—not even equipped with a telegraph. Servants were summoned by an archaic bell system that the president's mischievous sons knew precisely how to sabotage. Security was at best haphazard: an elderly doorkeeper, for instance, did little to screen the swarms of visitors who flooded the building daily, and so, on the staircases, a clerk recalled, "you could hardly squeeze your way up and down." As for sanitary facilities, the President's offices were equipped with but a single toilet. The rooms were drafty in winter and steaming in summer. When the windows were left open on hot evenings, huge bugs filled the rooms and tormented their occupants.

But such cramped quarters also encouraged intimacy, and the men and women who worked at the White House got to know the Lincolns well. Both his chief of staff and assistant clerk, for example, lived in a shared White House bedroom near the President's office, and got the chance to observe Lincoln firsthand day and night throughout the war. Not surprisingly, they later collaborated on the definitive nineteenth-century biography of the President.

Cabinet meetings took place in the same large room Lincoln used as his private office. Ministers sat around a long wooden table beneath an oil portrait of Andrew Jackson. And some—like Secretary of the Navy Gideon Welles and Secretary of the Treasury Salmon P. Chase— carefully recorded the official sessions in their diaries and were able later to reconstruct in postwar reminiscences the rather quaint ambience of the wartime White House.

In this mansion where the nation's future was secured, those who watched the "tall and forward-bending form" that paced the upper halls, "walking slowly, heavily, like a man in a dream," his "deep-set eyes . . . gazing far away, or into the future"—as Secretary William O. Stoddard recalls—were witness to both a national drama and a personal tragedy. ✣

"A Masculine Courage and Power"

JOHN G. NICOLAY

(1832–1901)

AND

JOHN M. HAY

(1838–1905)

PRIVATE SECRETARIES AND BIOGRAPHERS

Few intimates had the opportunity to observe the newly inaugurated President as closely as did his two chief White House assistants, Nicolay and Hay. The pair not only worked, but lived in the executive mansion and saw Lincoln daily throughout the Civil War. Years later they wrote a best-selling ten-volume history of the administration.

Mostly Hay and Nicolay present a highly idealized portrait of Lincoln, but in this excerpt the writers opened a revealing window onto a president who came close to buckling under the intense pressure of a feared Confederate invasion. Newly inaugurated, Lincoln had summoned troops to the defense of Washington shortly after the attack on Fort Sumter in April 1861. The call had elicited an outburst of enlistments. But for day after agonizing day, it did not bring sol-

diers to protect the capital. "Patriotism was paralyzed," the private secretaries remembered, "by the obstacle of a twenty miles' march" from
Annapolis. Nicolay and Hay—and Lincoln as well—wondered: "Had
the men of the North no legs?"

At one point during the crisis, Lincoln actually believed he heard
the roar of distant cannon and felt sure Washington was under attack.
When no one else could confirm the noise, Lincoln walked out onto
the street himself and anxiously asked passersby whether they had
heard the boom; no one had. The President sheepishly concluded that
it had been "a freak of his imagination." The troops finally arrived a few
days after the following scenes were observed by Nicolay and Hay. ✢

W E WERE THE DAILY AND NIGHTLY WITNESSES OF THE INCI-
DENTS, THE ANXIETIES, THE FEARS, AND THE HOPES
WHICH PERVADED THE EXECUTIVE MANSION AND THE
National Capital. . . .

Lincoln, by nature and habit so calm, so equable, so undemon-
strative, nevertheless passed this period of interrupted communication
and isolation from the North in a state of nervous tension which put
all his great powers of mental and physical endurance to their severest trial. General [Winfield] Scott's [general in chief of the federal
armies—ed.] reports, though invariably expressing his confidence in
successful defense, frankly admitted the evident danger; and the President, with his acuteness of observation and his rapidity and correct-
ness of inference, lost no single one of the external indications of
doubt and apprehension. Day after day prediction failed and hope was

deferred; troops did not come, ships did not arrive, railroads remained broken, messengers failed to reach their destination. That fact itself demonstrated that he was environed by the unknown—and that whether a Union or a Secession army would first reach the capital was at best an uncertainty.

To a coarse or vulgar nature such a situation would have brought only one of two feelings—either overpowering personal fear, or overweening bravado. But Lincoln, almost a giant in physical stature and strength, combined in his intellectual nature a masculine courage and power of logic with an ideal sensitiveness of conscience and a sentimental tenderness as delicate as a woman's. This Presidential trust which he had assumed was to him not a mere regalia of rank and honor. Its terrible duties and responsibilities seemed rather a coat of steel armor, heavy to bear, and cutting remorselessly into the quick flesh. That one of the successors of Washington should find himself even to this degree in the hands of his enemies was personally humiliating; but that the majesty of a great nation should be thus insulted and its visible symbols of authority be placed in jeopardy; above all, that the hitherto glorious example of the republic to other nations should stand in this peril of surprise and possible sudden collapse, the Constitution to be scoffed, and human freedom become a by-word and reproach— this must have begot in him an anxiety approaching torture.

In the eyes of his countrymen and of the world he was holding the scales of national destiny; he alone knew that for the moment the forces which made the beam vibrate with such uncertainty were beyond his control. In others' society he gave no sign of these inner emotions. But once, on the afternoon of the 23d, the business of the day being over, the Executive office deserted, after walking the floor alone in silent thought for nearly half an hour, he stopped and gazed long and wistfully out of the window down the Potomac in the direction of the expected ships; and, unconscious of other presence in the room, at length broke out with irrepressible anguish in the repeated exclamation, "Why don't they come! Why don't they come!"

One additional manifestation of this bitterness of soul occurred on the day following, though in a more subdued manner. The wounded soldiers of the Sixth Massachusetts [who had been attacked by civilian secession sympathizers as they passed through Baltimore— ed.], including several officers, came to pay a visit to the President. They were a little shy when they entered the room—having the traditional New England awe of authorities and rulers. Lincoln received them with sympathetic kindness which put them at ease after the interchange of the first greetings. His words of sincere thanks for their patriotism and their suffering, his warm praise of their courage, his hearty recognition of their great service to the public, and his earnestly expressed confidence in their further devotion, quickly won their trust. He spoke to them of the position and prospect of the city, contrasting their prompt arrival with the unexplained delay which seemed to have befallen the regiments supposed to be somewhere on their way from the various States. Pursuing this theme, he finally fell into a tone of irony to which only intense feeling ever drove him. "I begin to believe," said he, "that there is no North. The Seventh Regiment [of New York—ed.] is a myth. Rhode Island is another. You are the only real thing." There are few parchment brevets as precious as such a compliment, at such a time, from such a man.

"Wrapped in an Old Gray Shawl"

HENRY W. KNIGHT
(DATES UNKNOWN)
WAR DEPARTMENT GUARD

Knight served with the Sixth Corps of the Army of the Potomac and was in camp when President Lincoln arrived to review the troops in the spring of 1863, shortly before the Battle of Chancellorsville.

Like many soldiers who observed their commander in chief on such visits, young Knight was surprised by Lincoln's homespun appearance and seemingly graceless manner. Unlike most, however, Knight got the chance to learn much more about the President after he was wounded—and found himself assigned to guard duty at the War Department, where he encountered Lincoln dozens of times.

His recollections were first printed in *The Independent* in a special edition marking the thirtieth anniversary of Lincoln's death. ✣

I SEEM TO SEE HIM NOW, AS—HIS TALL, UNGAINLY FORM WRAPPED IN AN OLD GRAY SHAWL, WEARING USUALLY A "SHOCKINGLY BAD HAT," AND CARRYING A WORSE UMBRELLA—HE CAME UP THE STEPS into the building. Secretary [of War Edwin M.] Stanton, who knew Mr. Lincoln's midnight habits, gave a standing order that, although Mr. Lincoln might come from the White House alone (and he seldom came in any other way), he should never be permitted to return alone, but should be escorted by a file of four soldiers and a non-commissioned officer. I was on duty every other night. When Mr. Lincoln was ready to return we would take up a position near him, and accompany him safely to the White House. I presume I performed this duty fifty times. On the way to the White House, Mr. Lincoln would converse with us on various topics. I remember one night when it was raining very hard that he came over, and about one o'clock he started back. As he saw us at the door, ready to escort him, he addressed us in these words: "Don't come out in the storm with me tonight, boys. I have my umbrella, and can get home safely without you." "But," I replied, "Mr. President, we have positive orders from Mr. Stanton not to allow you to return alone; and you know we dare not disobey his orders." "No," replied Mr. Lincoln, "I suppose not; for if Stanton should learn that you had let me return alone, he would have you court-martialed and shot inside of twenty-four hours."

I recollect another very pleasing incident that took place in the same building. Those who may have been in the old War Department may remember that there were two short flights of stairs which had to be ascended in order to reach the second floor. At the head of the first flight was a platform or landing, and here the non-commissioned officer in charge of the guard had a desk and chair. Mr. Lincoln had to pass me whenever he came up these stairs, and as he did so I always arose, and, taking off my hat, remained standing till he passed. The taking-off of the hat was a mark of personal respect simply, for no soldier on duty, under any circumstances, is required to raise his hat. On one occasion, Mr. Lincoln, who always had a pleasant "Good-evening," and sometimes stopped to pass a word or two, hesitated on this landing, and, looking at the wall, where hung a pair of axes to be used in case of fire, asked what they were for. I replied that they were to be used in case of fire.

"Well, now," said he, "I wonder if I could lift one of those axes up by the end of the handle?" and, suiting the action to the word, he took one down, and, laying the heavy end on the floor, he commenced raising it till he held it out at arm's length, and kept it there several seconds. "I thought I could do it," he said, as he put it down. "You try it." I did try it, and failed. Mr. Lincoln laughed, and as he passed on he said: "When I used to split rails, thirty years ago in Illinois, I could lift two axes that way; and I believe I could do it now, and I will try it some other time."

"His Grief Unnerved Him"

ELIZABETH KECKLEY

(1818–1901)

MRS. LINCOLN'S DRESSMAKER

A pre-war employee of Mrs. Jefferson Davis, seamstress "Lizzie" Keckley became the self-styled White House "modiste" in 1861, when the Davises moved south to the Confederacy and the Lincolns moved east to Washington. Keckley, a former slave, had purchased her own freedom and established herself as a dressmaker whose skill with a needle was equaled by her keen sense of style. Eventually, when Mrs. Lincoln's high-strung temperament drove away most of her Washington lady friends, Keckley also became her closest confidante.

Her 1868 memoir, *Behind the Scenes, or Thirty Years a Slave and Four Years in the White House*, infuriated Mrs. Lincoln, who never spoke to her again. Although it was ghostwritten, it surely drew on Keckley's still-vivid memories of her days with the family. The following excerpts from the book run the gamut from family despair to joviality, recalling a couple facing personal tragedy and, like many ordinary couples, personal jealousy as well. ✣

SHE WAS EXTREMELY JEALOUS OF HIM, AND IF A LADY DESIRED TO COURT HER DISPLEASURE, SHE COULD SELECT NO SURER WAY TO DO IT THAN TO PAY MARKED ATTENTION TO THE President. These little jealous freaks often were a source of perplexity to Mr. Lincoln. If it was a reception for which they were dressing, he would come into her room to conduct her down-stairs, and while pulling on his gloves ask, with a merry twinkle in his eyes:

"Well, mother, who must I talk with to-night—shall it be Mrs. D.?"

"That deceitful woman! No, you shall not listen to her flattery."

"Well, then, what do you say to Miss C.? She is too young and handsome to practise deceit."

"Young and handsome, you call her! You should not judge beauty for me. No, she is in league with Mrs. D., and you shall not talk with her."

"Well, mother, I must talk with some one. Is there any one that you do not object to?" trying to button his glove, with a mock expression of gravity.

"I don't know as it is necessary that you should speak to anybody in particular. You know well enough, Mr. Lincoln, that I do not approve of your flirtations with silly women, just as if you were a beardless boy, fresh from school."

"But, mother, I insist that I must talk with somebody. I can't stand around like a simpleton, and say nothing. If you will not tell me who I may talk with, please tell me who I may *not* talk with."

"There is Mrs. D. and Miss C. in particular. I detest them both. Mrs. B. also will come around you, but you need not listen to her flattery. These are the ones in particular."

"Very well, mother; now that we have settled the question to your satisfaction, we will go down-stairs;" and always with stately dignity he proffered his arm and led the way. . . .

The reception [an 1862 White House levee—ed.] was a large and brilliant one, and the rich notes of the Marine Band in the apartments below came to the sick-room in soft, subdued murmurs, like the wild, faint sobbing of far-off spirits. Some of the young people had suggested dancing, but Mr. Lincoln met the suggestion with an emphatic veto. The brilliance of the scene could not dispel the sadness that rested upon the face of Mrs. Lincoln. During the evening she came up-stairs several times, and stood by the bedside of the suffering boy. She loved him with a mother's heart, and her anxiety was great. The night passed slowly; morning came, and Willie was worse. He lingered a few days, and died. God called the beautiful spirit home, and the house of joy was turned into the house of mourning. I was worn out with the watching, and was not in the room when Willie died, but was immediately sent for. I assisted in washing him and dressing him, and then laid him on the bed, when Mr. Lincoln came in. I never saw a man so bowed down with grief. He came to the bed, lifted the cover from the face of his child, gazed at it long and earnestly, murmuring, "My poor boy, he was too good for this earth. God has called him home. I know that he is much better off in heaven, but then we loved him so. It is hard, hard to have him die!"

Great sobs choked his utterance. He buried his head in his hands, and his tall frame was convulsed with emotion. I stood at the foot of the bed, my eyes full of tears, looking at the man in silent, awe-stricken wonder. His grief unnerved him, and make him a weak, passive child. I did not dream that his rugged nature could be so moved. I shall never forget those solemn moments—genius and greatness weeping over love's idol lost.

"This Gently Smiling Father"

JULIA TAFT (BAYNE)

(1845–?)

SONS' BABY-SITTER

Julia was the daughter of Horatio N. Taft, chief examiner of the federal patent office. In 1861 her young brothers, Bud and Holly, became chums of the Lincoln boys, Willie and Tad. Julia often accompanied them to the White House to supervise their merry, sometimes raucous, play. But the Taft family's close relationship with the Lincolns ended abruptly with Willie's death from typhoid fever in February 1862. Bud and Holly were all but banished from the White House because, Mary Lincoln later explained, the sight of them proved too "painful" for the grieving Tad.

In her eighties, Julia assembled her "girlhood memories" into a memoir, which she entitled, *Tad Lincoln's Father*. They provide an important glimpse of some of the rare, happy moments in the presidential household in wartime Washington before Willie's death plunged the family into despair. ✢

I F THERE WAS ANY MOTTO OR SLOGAN OF THE WHITE HOUSE DURING THE EARLY YEARS OF THE LINCOLNS' OCCUPANCY IT WAS THIS: "LET THE CHILDREN HAVE A GOOD TIME." OFTEN I HAVE heard Mrs. Lincoln say this with a smile, as her two sons and my two brothers rushed tumultuously through the room, talking loudly of some plan for their amusement.

And no less smiling and gracious was the tall, spare man, half of us called "Pa" and the rest of us (as we were taught at home) "Mist' Pres'dent," with no thought of its high import—this gently smiling father who played with us and told us stories when those whom Tad called "plaguey old generals" gave him a little leisure.

When the President came into the family sitting room and sat down to read, the boys would rush at him and demand a story. Tad perched precariously on the back of the big chair, Willie on one knee, Bud on the other, both leaning against him. Holly usually found a place on the arm of the chair, and often I would find myself swept into the group by the long arm which seemed to reach almost across the room.

I wish I could remember some of those stories. Usually they were melodramatic tales of hunters and settlers attacked by Indians. I have thought since that some of these tales may have been based on actual occurrences in the President's boyhood and I am sorry that my memory is so dim concerning them. I am afraid the boys enjoyed them more than I did. At the close of one favorite story of frontiersmen chased by the Indians, he would drawl impressively, "they galloped and galloped, with the redskins close behind."

"But they got away, Pa, they got away," interrupted Tad.

"Oh, yes, they got away." Then suddenly rising to his full height, "Now I must get away."

Whenever I see St. Gaudens' statue of Lincoln, I think of these story hours and my memory supplies the four little wriggling figures, all gone now.

President Lincoln liked to play with the boys whenever he had a little time from his duties. Willie used to say mournfully, "Pa don't have time to play with us now." Once I heard a terrible racket in another room, and opening the door with the idea of bestowing some sisterly "don't" upon my young brothers, whose voices could be heard amid the din, beheld the President lying on the floor, with the four boys trying to hold him down. Willie and Bud had hold of his hands, Holly and Tad sprawled over his feet and legs, while the broad grin of Mr. Lincoln's face was evidence that he was enjoying himself hugely. As soon as the boys saw my face at the door, Tad called, "Julie, come quick and sit on his stomach." But this struck me too much like laying profane hands on the Lord's anointed, and I closed the door and went out.

You may infer from the part I played in some of these incidents that I was a conceited little prig. But I really don't think I was. I was dignified with the weight of sixteen years, remember, although the President always treated me as though I was about half that age, and many of the pranks of my young brothers and the Lincoln boys deeply shocked my sense of propriety. . . .

Late one afternoon I was curled up in the window of the sitting room, looking at a large book, when the President came in. I jumped to my feet.

He said, "How is Julie to-day? Sit down, child."

I was glad to do so for the book I was clasping was heavy. He took it from me, turned over the leaves absently, then put it on my lap, saying, "Such a big book for little Julie."

Resting one hand on my shoulder and the other on the window above my head, he looked long and earnestly over the Long Bridge into Virginia and sighed heavily. Then he walked up and down, up and down the long room, his hands behind him and his head bent, sighing now and then. I think he had entirely forgotten my presence. He looked so sad and worried that somehow I wanted to comfort him yet knew not how. And crying a little, I slipped out in the darkening twilight.

President Lincoln always appeared to me well dressed. I am sure I should have noticed otherwise, for I was a rather particular young person in regard to such things. And he never appeared awkward to me. My father was inclined to be critical in matters of etiquette but he said he never saw Lincoln embarrassed in greeting foreigners of distinction. "The President seems anxious to make every one comfortable and at their ease," remarked my father, "which is the essence of good breeding."

Once, as I was sitting on the sofa with some silk and velvet pieces on my lap, out of which I was trying to make a pin-cushion, the President came into the room. I rose at once, my pieces falling on the floor. When the President went out, I picked them up and was just getting them sorted out again when he came in the second time. True to my training, I again rose and the silk once more scattered to the floor.

"You needn't get up, Julia, every time Abram comes in the room," said Mrs. Lincoln.

"Why, Julie," said the President, noticing my silk pieces on the floor, "that's too bad." Before I knew what he was about, he had knelt on the floor and was picking up the pieces of silk for me. Greatly embarrassed at this presidential gallantry, I darted forward to help him and together we picked them up.

One day the boys and I, who should have known better, were leaning out of the front windows to watch a regiment go by, when the President passed and pulled us all in. He jerked in the boys with little ceremony but lifted me down gently, saying, "Do you want to break your neck, honey? . . ."

Another time I was in the sitting room with Mrs. Lincoln when the President came in with a bunch of photographs in his hand. They were new pictures of himself, and he and Mrs. Lincoln looked them over and commented on the different poses. Then he turned to me saying, "Julie do you want my picture?"

"Oh, yes, sir," I said eagerly, for indeed I wanted one.

"Give me a kiss then and you can have it," he agreed. So I stretched up and he leaned over and I gave him a peck on the cheek. I remember to this day how scratchy his whiskers were.

He drew me to him, saying, "Now we will pick out a good one," and I still have the one we finally selected.

Whatever I think of Mr. Lincoln, I see him sprawled out in that big chair in the sitting room, for it was there that I came most in contact with him. I remember going to that room one morning rather early, looking for Mrs. Lincoln or the boys, and finding the President there alone in his big chair with the old, worn Bible on his lap. He spoke to me in an absent-minded sort of a way and clasping my hand, rested it on his knee, as I stood by him. He seemed to see something interesting out of the window. I stood there for what seemed to me a long time, with my hand clasped in his. I followed his gaze out of the window but could see nothing but the tops of some trees. I thought it wouldn't be polite for me to pull my hand out of his grasp, even if I could, so I stood there until my arm fairly ached. Why did I not ask him what he saw out there? I think he would have told me. Finally he turned to me with a look of startled surprise and said,

"Why, Julie, have I been holding you here all this time?" He released me and I went off to find the boys.

"He Had a Vast Capacity for Work"

WILLIAM OSBORN STODDARD

(1835–1925)

WHITE HOUSE CLERK

A young pro-Lincoln journalist from Illinois who became the third White House secretary in 1861, Stoddard spent nearly three years supervising the President's incoming mail—reading letters, forwarding requests for action by government departments, preparing news summaries, and passing along a selection of each day's correspondence to Lincoln for review and reply. The mail, Stoddard later recalled, arrived daily "in bales."

A gifted writer, Stoddard began producing reminiscences of Lincoln only a few months after the assassination and maintained a remarkable output of books for decades to come—volumes like *Inside the White House in War Times* (1890), *The Table Talk of Abraham Lincoln* (1894), and *Lincoln at Work: Sketches from Life* (1900). Among Stoddard's least-known but most vivid recollections is this account of Lincoln's agony following the catastrophic Union defeat at the Battle of Chancellorsville. It is excerpted from an 1895 anthology entitled *Abraham Lincoln: Tributes from His Associates,* edited by Rev. William Hayes Ward. ❖

LINCOLN'S CHARACTERISTIC AS A WORKER WAS HIS PERSIS-
TENCY, HIS TIRELESSNESS; AND FOR THIS HE WAS ENDOWED
WITH RARE TOUGHNESS OF BODILY AND MENTAL FIBRE. THERE
was not a weak spot in his whole animal organism, and his brain was
thoroughly healthy; his White House life, therefore, was a continual
stepping from one duty to another. There was also what to a host of
men was a provoking way of stepping over or across unessential
things, with an instinctive perception of their lack of value. Some
things that he stepped over seemed vastly important to those who had
them in hand, but at the same time he discovered real importances
where others failed to see them.

He had vast capacity for work, and also the exceedingly valuable
faculty of putting work upon others. He could load, up to their limit
or beyond it, his Cabinet officers, generals, legislative supporters, and
so forth. He could hold them responsible, sharply; but he never really
interfered with them, "bothered them," at their work, or found undue
fault with its execution. A false idea obtained circulation at one time
concerning his hardness, his exacting dealings with his immediate co-
workers and subordinates. Perhaps this arose from the numerous
changes made in his civil and military appointments. He was the very
reverse of exacting. For illustration, I do not know or believe that he
ever found fault with one of his private secretaries in all the onerous
and delicate duties with which they were charged. I know that during
all the years of my own service he never uttered a criticism or ex-

pressed a disapproval, and yet such a mass of work could not possibly have all been perfect. He was the most kindly and lenient of men, even when, through days and days of gloom and overwork, he would pass us, invariably, without speaking, as if we were not there, until business gave us the right to speak.

Did he never at any time reel or stagger under his burden? Oh yes, once. He could feel a hit or a stab at any time, but the things which hurt him, that made him suffer, that were slowly killing him, as he himself declared, did not interfere with the perpetual efficiency of his work. If there were hours when despondency came and when he doubted the result, the final triumph of the national arms, he did not tell anybody; but there was one night when his wrestle with despair was long and terrible.

In the opinion of Edwin M. Stanton, concurred in by other good judges, the darkest hour of the Civil War came in the first week of May, 1863. The Army of the Potomac, under General Hooker, had fought the bloody battle of Chancellorsville. The record of their dead and wounded told how bravely they had fought; but they were defeated, losing the field of battle, and seventeen thousand men. The Confederate commanders acknowledged a loss of only thirteen thousand, but their Army of Northern Virginia was dreadfully cut up. How severe a disaster this costly victory had been to them could not be understood by the people of the North.

The country was weary of the long war, with its draining taxes of gold and blood. Discontent was everywhere raising its head, and the opponents of the Lincoln administration were savage in their denunciations. Many of his severest critics were men of unquestionable patriotism. The mail desk in the Secretary's office at the White House was heaped with letters, as if the President could read them. He knew their purport well enough without reading. He knew of the forever vacant places in a hundred thousand households before Chancellorsville. . . .

That night, the last visitors in Lincoln's room were Stanton and [General Henry W.] Halleck. They went away together in silence, at somewhere near nine o'clock, and the President was left alone. Not another soul was on that floor except the one secretary, who was busy with the mail in his room across the hall from the President's; and the doors of both rooms were ajar, for the night was warm. The silence was so deep that the ticking of a clock would have been noticeable; but another sound came that was almost as regular and ceaseless. It was the tread of the President's feet as he strode slowly back and forth across the chamber in which so many Presidents of the United States had done their work. Was he to be the last of the line? The last President of the entire United States? At that hour that very question had been asked of him by the battle of Chancellorsville. If he had wavered, if he had failed in faith or courage or prompt decision, then the nation, and not the Army of the Potomac, would have lost its great battle.

Ten o'clock came, without a break in the steady march, excepting now and then a pause in turning at either wall. There was an unusual accumulation of letters, for that was a desk hard worked with other duties also, and it was necessary to clear it before leaving it. It seemed as if they contained a double allowance of denunciation, threats, ribaldry. Some of them were hideous, some were tear-blistered. Some would have done Lincoln good if he could have read them; but, over there in his room, he was reading the lesson of Chancellorsville and the future of the Republic.

Eleven o'clock came, and then another hour of that ceaseless march so accustomed the ear to it that when, a little after twelve, there was a break of several minutes, the sudden silence made one put down letters and listen.

The President may have been at his table writing, or he may—no man knows or can guess; but at the end of the minutes, long or short, the tramp began again. Two o'clock, and he was walking yet, and when, a little after three, the secretary's task was done and he slipped noiselessly out, he turned at the head of the stairs for a moment. It was so—the last sound he heard as he went down was the footfall in Lincoln's room.

That was not all, however. The young man had need to return early, and he was there again before eight o'clock. The President's room door was open and he went in. There sat Mr. Lincoln eating breakfast alone. He had not been out of his room; but there was a kind of cheery, hopeful, morning light on his face, instead of the funereal battle-cloud from Chancellorsville. He had watched all night, but a dawn had come, for beside his cup of coffee lay the written draft of his instructions to General Hooker to push forward, to fight again. There was a decisive battle won that night in that long vigil with disaster and despair. Only a few weeks later the Army of the Potomac fought it over again as desperately—and they won it—at Gettysburg.

"The President Came to the Office Every Day"

————◆————

THOMAS T. ECKERT

(1825–1910)

CHIEF OF WAR DEPARTMENT TELEGRAPH OFFICE

An experienced telegraph operator, the Ohio-born Eckert volunteered when war broke out and was soon serving as chief of the War Department telegraph office. Lincoln was a frequent visitor, especially during military movements, when he was hungry for information from the field, and he grew friendly with several of the operators. But the President developed the closest relationship with Major Eckert, whom he would later send on a sensitive mission to confer with Confederate leaders seeking an armistice. In 1862, Eckert claimed, Lincoln wrote the first draft of his Emancipation Proclamation in the relative quiet of the telegraph office, using paper supplied by Eckert himself. The major later provided details of this experience to David Homer Bates, who was writing *Lincoln in the Telegraph Office*. This is the full recollection.

Eckert—who was invited to join the Lincolns at Ford's Theatre the night of the assassination but, to his lifelong regret, declined—became, in later years, appropriately enough, president of Western Union. ✢

As you know, the President came to the office every day and invariably sat at my desk while there. Upon his arrival early one morning in June, 1862, shortly after McClellan's "Seven Days' Fight," he asked me for some paper, as he wanted to write something special. I procured some foolscap and handed it to him. He then sat down and began to write. I do not recall whether the sheets were loose or had been made into a pad. There must have been at least a quire. He would look out of the window a while and then put his pen to paper, but he did not write much at once. He would study between times and when he had made up his mind he would put down a line or two, and then sit quiet for a few minutes. After a time he would resume his writing, only to stop again at intervals to make some remark to me or to one of the cipher-operators as a fresh despatch from the front was handed to him.

Once his eye was arrested by the sight of a large spider-web stretched from the lintel of the portico to the side of the outer window-sill. This spider-web was an institution of the cipher-room and harbored a large colony of exceptionally big ones. We frequently watched their antics, and Assistant Secretary Watson dubbed them "Major Eckert's lieutenants." Lincoln commented on the web, and I told him that my lieutenants would soon report and pay their respects to the President. Not long after a big spider appeared at the cross-roads and tapped several times on the strands, whereupon five or six others came out from different directions. Then what seemed to be a great confab took place, after which they separated, each on a different strand of the web. Lincoln was much interested in the performance and thereafter, while working at the desk, would often watch for the appearance of his visitors.

On the first day Lincoln did not cover one sheet of his special writing paper (nor indeed on any subsequent day). When ready to leave, he asked me to take charge of what he had written and not allow any one to see it. I told him I would do this with pleasure and would not read it myself. "Well," he said, "I should be glad to know that no one will see it, although there is no objection to your looking at it; but please keep it locked up until I call for it to-morrow." I said his wishes would be strictly complied with.

When he came to the office on the following day he asked for the papers, and I unlocked my desk and handed them to him and he again sat down to write. This he did nearly every day for several weeks, always handing me what he had written when ready to leave the office each day. Sometimes he would not write more than a line or two, and once I observed that he had put question-marks on the margin of what he had written. He would read over each day all the matter he had previously written and revise it, studying carefully each sentence.

On one occasion he took the papers away with him, but he brought them back a day or two later. I became much interested in the matter and was impressed with the idea that he was engaged upon something of great importance, but did not know what it was until he had finished the document and then for the first time he told me that he had been writing an order giving freedom to the slaves in the South, for the purpose of hastening the end of the war. He said he had been able to work at my desk more quietly and command his thoughts better than at the White House, where he was frequently interrupted. I still have in my possession the ink-stand which he used at that time and which, as you know, stood on my desk until after Lee's surrender. The pen he used was a small barrel-pen made by Gillott—such as were supplied to the cipher-operators.

"I Made the Promise to Myself"

SALMON P. CHASE

(1808–1863)

SECRETARY OF THE TREASURY

Senator Chase had been Ohio's favorite son at the 1860 Republican Convention, but lost the nomination to Lincoln. He was compensated with an appointment to head the Treasury Department, which he proceeded to manage efficiently, imaginatively, and incorruptibly for more than three years. Arguably, the Union war effort could not have been pursued without Chase's skill in financing it.

But Chase never abandoned his presidential aspirations. He clashed repeatedly with Lincoln over political patronage, and then encouraged speculation in 1864 that he was available to replace Lincoln at the top of the national ticket. Having "reached a point of mutual embarrassment in our official relation," Lincoln accepted Chase's resignation in June 1864. Six months later, safely reelected, the President surprised many Republicans by appointing Chase chief justice of the Supreme Court.

Chase kept a diary during his years in the Lincoln administration, from which the following entry is drawn. It recalls the historic cabinet meeting of 22 September 1862 at which the President announced that he was issuing an Emancipation Proclamation. The account remains the best record we will ever have of those nation-changing moments. ✤

ALL THE MEMBERS OF THE CABINET WERE IN ATTENDANCE. THERE WAS SOME GENERAL TALK AND THE PRESIDENT MENTIONED THAT ARTEMUS WARD [ONE OF LINCOLN'S FAVORITE humorists—ed.] had sent him his book. Proposed to read a chapter which he thought very funny. Read it, and seemed to enjoy it very much—the Heads also (except Stanton) of course. The Chapter was "High-handed Outrage at Utica."

The President then took a graver tone and said:

"Gentlemen; I have, as you are aware, thought a great deal about the relation of this war to Slavery; and you all remember that, several weeks ago, I read to you an Order I had prepared on this subject, which, on account of objections made by some of you, was not issued.

Ever since then, my mind has been much occupied with this subject, and I have thought all along that the time for acting on it might probably come. I think the time has come now. I wish it were a better time. I wish that we were in a better condition. The action of the army against the rebels has not been quite what I should have best liked. But they have been driven out of Maryland [at the Battle of Antietam five days earlier—ed.], and Pennsylvania is no longer in danger of invasion. When the rebel army was at Frederick, I determined, as soon as it should be driven out of Maryland, to issue a Proclamation of Emancipation such as I thought most likely to be useful. I said nothing to any one; but I made the promise to myself, and (hesitating a little)—to my Maker. The rebel army is now driven out, and I am going to fulfill that promise. I have got you together to hear what I have written down. I do not wish your advice about the main matter—for that I have determined for myself. This I say without intending anything but respect for any one of you. But I already know the views of each on this question. They have been heretofore expressed, and I have considered them as thoroughly and carefully as I can. What I have written is that which my reflections have determined me to say. If there is anything in the expressions I use, or in any other minor matter, which any one of you thinks had best be changed, I shall be glad to receive the suggestions. One other observation I will make. I know very well that many others might, in this matter, as in others, do better than I can; and if I were satisfied that the public confidence was more fully possessed by any one of them than by me, and knew of any

Constitutional way in which he could be put in my place, he should have it. I would gladly yield it to him. But though I believe that I have not so much of the confidence of the people as I had some time since, I do not know that, all things considered, any other person has more; and, however this may be, there is no way in which I can have any other man put where I am. I am here. I must do the best I can, and bear the responsibility of taking the course which I feel I ought to take."

The President then proceeded to read his Emancipation Proclamation, making remarks on the several parts as he went on, and showing that he had fully considered the whole subject, in all the lights under which it had been presented to him. . . .

I followed saying: "What you have said, Mr. President, fully satisfies me that you have given to every proposition which has been made, a kind and candid consideration. And you have now expressed the conclusion to which you have arrived, clearly and distinctly. This it was your right, and under your oath of office your duty, to do. The Proclamation does not, indeed, mark out exactly the course I should myself prefer. But I am ready to take it just as it is written, and to stand by it with all my heart."

"So Great Was the Pressure"

WILLIAM H. CROOK

(1839–1915)

BODYGUARD

A Union army veteran, Crook was serving on Washington's municipal police force when he was assigned in January 1865 to guard the White House. He became one of several plainclothes policemen working round the clock to provide security for the President. Crook was well suited for the job—in his own words, "wiry, lithe, and powerful . . . knowing what nerves meant, with clear eyesight, keen sense of hearing, and ready to go anywhere or do anything at a moment's notice."

At first Crook was assigned the 4 P.M.–midnight shift, and later the midnight–8 A.M. shift, seated in a chair outside Lincoln's bedroom to guard him while he slept. Eventually, the bodyguard graduated to daytime duty. In each assignment, he reported "to the President *personally*."

During his three months with Lincoln, Crook observed the family firsthand on many occasions. Evidently he did his job well, for he continued to serve in the White House in various capacities through the administration of Theodore Roosevelt. Then, in 1911, Crook published a memoir of his White House experiences, as told to an editor named Henry Rood. Thus, the resulting recollections are not contemporaneous with his service under Lincoln and come down to us secondhand through the interpretations of an interviewer. But they constitute a valuable view of the executive mansion during the waning days of the Civil War, from the unique perspective of one pledged—but in the end unable—to prevent any harm coming to Abraham Lincoln. ✤

A T ABOUT EIGHT-THIRTY HE WOULD JOIN MRS. LINCOLN AND LITTLE TAD IN THE SMALL, UNPRETENTIOUS DINING-ROOM FOR BREAKFAST, WHERE A PLAIN BUT SUFFICIENTLY HEARTY meal was served by two waiters who were white men, and who were paid personally by the President, who also paid the wages of the cook and his coachman and footman. There was little formality about the meal; the President loved to joke with his wife and son, and for the time being put aside the cares of his great office and his anxiety for the country. As soon as breakfast was over, the President would go to his office and commence the ceaseless toil of his busy day. . . .

Mr. Lincoln ate heartily but not to excess; he was particularly fond of certain things, especially apples, and Mrs. Lincoln always had a sufficiency of this fruit chosen carefully and ready at hand. The President never used tobacco as far as I know, and I never knew him to drink wine or other alcoholic beverages, not even at the state dinners where, of course, wines were provided for those who wished them. I am quite sure that neither he nor Mrs. Lincoln worried about the possibility of the President being assassinated. Certainly if Mrs. Lincoln was worried about such an occurrence she did not show it, and the President exercised the calm philosophy of a stoic in this particular. He believed that if anybody was bad enough to kill him there was nothing on earth to prevent it. . . .

Again, I remind my readers of the fact that during Lincoln's administration the country was torn apart with the most terrible warfare; death was on every hand, the black badge of mourning was seen on every side; and those connected with the White House, where centered the entire nervous system of the nation, felt the strain of conflict, the grief and sorrow, so poignantly and so constantly that it is no wonder gayety and lightness of spirit were absent for the most part. Then again, the President's second son, Willie Lincoln, had died only two years previous [in fact, Willie had died three years earlier—ed.], and both President and Mrs. Lincoln unquestionably felt this loss while I was acting as body-guard. . . .

At that time, it must be remembered, any one who wished to talk with Lincoln could walk up to his office, and after speaking with the doorkeeper go in and meet him. Excepting when engaged with others, President Lincoln seldom if ever declined to receive any man or woman who came to the White House to see him. When I remember the numbers of people who came there on all conceivable errands, for all imaginable purposes, it seems surprising that he could get through with his work and then grant them interviews. But Lincoln had a most effective way of dismissing those who trespassed upon his time, which belonged not to himself but to the nation. Let me give an illustration of what I mean.

Some morning an up-state politician would come bustling into the White House and want to see the President, not for any good reason, but merely that he might go back to his constituents and tell how he was received by the President, and what he said to the President, and what the President said to him, etc. etc.

Lincoln would size up such a man in half a minute, and he could get rid of him in another half minute, not brusquely, not by waving him aside, not by suggesting that he was too busy to be seen at that particular time; on the contrary, before the up-state politician would have a chance to tell what he thought of the President's policies Mr. Lincoln would start in on a droll story, and when he finished the politician would be laughing so heartily he would forget all about what he was going to tell the President. Then his hand would be grasped by the President, who would at once turn to his desk, and the politician would find himself leaving the White House more than satisfied with his call, which had lasted two minutes instead of two hours as he had expected.

So great was the pressure on the President's time and thought that he had little chance for pleasure and recreation, except for an occasional horseback ride out to the Soldiers Home. He enjoyed moderately a really good theatrical performance by competent actors, but not with the enthusiasm shown by Mrs. Lincoln, who was very fond indeed of the drama. When the President and his wife went to the theater, they would step into a carriage at the White House and drive directly to their destination, just as any other gentleman and lady in private life would do. On arriving in front of the playhouse Burke, the big, burly Irish coachman, would pull up his horses, and the footman, Charley Forbes, would swing down to the sidewalk and open the door of the carriage, whereupon Mrs. Lincoln and the President would step out, being met at once by a body-guard whose business it was to be on hand when they arrived.

Without any ostentation or display whatever the President and Mrs. Lincoln, followed by the body-guard, and led by an usher, would quietly walk into the box which had been reserved for them, and as they did so the audience would rise and stand in silence until the President acknowledged this mark of respect with a dignified bow, in which recognition Mrs. Lincoln joined by a graceful inclination of her head. Then they would seat themselves in the box and the audience would seat itself throughout the house. During the progress of the play the attention of the audience was centered on the stage and not upon the President and his wife, or any guests whom they might have with them in the box; for Lincoln was so near to the people of his beloved country that they felt no desire to stare at him from motives of curiosity. At the conclusion of the play, Mr. and Mrs. Lincoln and their guard would retire from the box, and quietly leave the theater. Such of the audience as were in the aisles simply made way for them. They would then step into their carriage, Forbes would close the door and regain his seat beside Burke, who would speak to his horses and away the carriage would roll toward the White House as a score of other carriages were rolling in other directions from the theater. . . .

There was no hilarity excepting where Tad was concerned. Time and time again have I seen Tad sitting on his father's shoulders, while

President Lincoln galloped up and down the long corridor outside their private apartments, the boy laughing with glee, and the great, grave President, by sheer will-power, resolutely throwing aside the burdens of his office, in order that his little son might share the joys that are childhood's heritage. . . .

As he went upstairs and entered his own room, Lincoln's last act was to turn to the guard on duty in the corridor, and wish him good-night. Then he would enter his room, and close the door, and I—if it were my turn to stand guard—would settle down for eight hours of duty.

My chair stood in the corridor, within easy reach of the door opening into the President's room, and so situated that I could see every inch of the whole length of the corridor, which was lighted that no shadows could even partly conceal any one who might try to slip through it. During most of the night I would rest comfortably in the chair, constantly looking this way and that, listening intently for any unusual noise. Every once in a while, however, I would rise and quietly pace up and down to obtain rest of position. I never read a book or a newspaper, of course, for fear that my attention might become fixed so closely on the printed page that I might not hear or see the approach of assassins whom I always expected at any moment. Needless to say, I never resorted to any of the common means for keeping awake during those solitary vigils. The responsibility of guarding Lincoln was so great that dozing, or even drowsiness, was unthinkable. And when relieved by the day guard, at eight o'clock in the morning,

I was always as fresh and wide awake as when I had gone on duty twelve hours previous.

The only time that President Lincoln failed to say good-night to me—when we parted after having been together for hours—was on the evening shortly before he started for Ford's Theater, where he was murdered. As I mentioned on another occasion, some years ago, Mr. Lincoln had told me that afternoon of a dream he had had for three successive nights, concerning his impending assassination. Of course, the constant dread of such a calamity made me somewhat nervous, and I almost begged him to remain in the Executive Mansion that night, and not to go to the theater. But he would not disappoint Mrs. Lincoln and others who were to be present. Then I urged that he allow me to stay on duty and accompany him; but he would not hear of this either.

"No, Crook," he said kindly but firmly, "you have had a long, hard day's work already, and must go home to sleep and rest. I cannot afford to have you get all tired out and exhausted."

It was then that he neglected, for the first and only time, to say good-night to me. Instead, he turned, with his kind, grave face and said: "Good-bye, Crook," and went into his room.

I thought of it at the moment; and a few hours later, when the awful news flashed over Washington that he had been shot, his last words were so burned into my memory that they never have been forgotten, and never can be forgotten.

Although I have already stated the fact in print, I wish to repeat it here—that when Mr. and Mrs. Lincoln and their party sat down in their box at Ford's Theater that fateful night, the guard who was acting as my substitute [John F. Parker—ed.] took his position at the rear of the box, close to an entrance leading into the box from the dress-circle of the theater. His orders were to stand there, fully armed, and to permit no unauthorized person to pass into the box. His orders were to stand there and protect the President at all hazards.

From the spot where he was thus stationed, this guard could not see the stage or the actors; but he could hear the words the actors spoke, and he became so interested in them that, incredible as it may seem, he quietly deserted his post of duty, and walking down the dimly-lighted side aisle, deliberately took a seat in the last row of the dress-circle.

It was while the President was thus absolutely unprotected through this guard's amazing recklessness—to use no stronger words—that Booth rushed through the entrance to the box, just deserted by the guard, and accomplished his foul deed.

Realization of his part in the assassination so preyed upon the mind and spirit of the guard that he finally died as a result of it.

A NOTE ON EDITORIAL METHODS

Much of the material in this volume comes from out-of-print books of the nineteenth century, and magazines and newspapers published during Lincoln's lifetime, or in the months and years immediately following his assassination.

Generally, little editorial intervention was imposed on these reminiscences, although in the few clashes between archaic spellings and modern, computerized spell-check variations, I have generally allowed the newer technologies to rule, for the sake of consistency and readability. I have also broken up the occasional interminable paragraph and adopted standardized capitalization. And sometimes I have corrected punctuation and expanded abbreviations—as in the memory from Dennis Hanks, whose distinctive style of writing is difficult for modern readers to parse.

Other recollections come from original manuscripts (typographical errors intact) or from diary material and transcriptions replete with eccentric punctuation and arcane spelling. In such cases I have made the changes necessary to create a uniform style for the text. The ubiquitous ampersand has routinely been changed to "and," for example, and abbreviations replaced by more formal descriptions ("President" instead of "Presdt," for instance). The occasional reference to "Jeff. Davis" has been standardized as "Jefferson Davis."

Long dashes that once concluded sentences have been replaced by periods, and commas inserted or deleted as necessary (but mostly deleted—Mary Lincoln was but one of many "writers" of her day who believed that unless a sentence was filled with commas, it must be improperly composed). Similarly, the once-ubiquitous comma, followed by a dash, has been simplified, and where British-style single-quotation marks once routinely alternated with double-quotes, the modern American style has been used throughout the book.

It is important to point out that with the imposition of these changes, however subtle, the selections no longer qualify as precise transcriptions suitable for scholarly research. But in their edited format, each introduced by a biographical sketch of the contributor, they preserve the spirit of their subject, their authors, and the era in which they were composed.

The reminiscences might have been presented chronologically—based on the approximate time of each recollector's initial exposure to the subject—thus allowing Lincoln to emerge, change, and grow, precisely as he did over the course of years in life. But it soon became evident that a significant number of eyewitnesses had known Lincoln for too long, through too many changes in the subject's life, to make it possible to compress their evolving impressions of the man into chapters framed by time alone (although Lincoln was also known to drop longtime acquaintances once he outgrew them, especially after he assumed the presidency). The choice was made instead to group the reminiscences by category, allowing family, friends, fellow attorneys, military men, and White House staff, to name a few, to speak in groups.

Finally, wherever possible, I kept all copyediting to a minimum and inserted editorial notes sparingly. The recollectors, who knew Abraham Lincoln, should be allowed to speak again for themselves, just as they did as long as a century and a quarter ago, and wherever possible, I have allowed them to do so freely.

NOTES FROM THE INTRODUCTION

1. William H. Herndon and Jesse K. Weik, *Herndon's Lincoln: The True Story of a Great Life,* Vol. III (Chicago: Belford-Clark, 1889), p. 441.

2. Herbert Mitgang, ed., *Edward Dicey's Spectator of America* (Chicago: Quadrangle Books, 1971), p. 92; Arthur Schlesinger Jr., "The Ultimate Approval Rating," *New York Times Magazine* (15 December 1996), p. 46.

3. Herndon's and Nicolay's interviews were recently published as books. See Douglas L. Wilson and Rodney O. Davis, *Herndon's Informants: Letters, Interviews, and Statements about Abraham Lincoln* (Champaign: University of Illinois Press, 1998), and Michael Burlingame, ed., *An Oral History of Abraham Lincoln: John G. Nicolay's Interviews and Essays* (Carbondale: Southern Illinois University Press, 1996).

4. White House correspondence clerk William Osborn Stoddard, for example, made a cottage industry of Lincoln, producing a virtual shelf of books during his long life. See, especially, *Inside the White House in War Times* (New York: Charles L. Webster & Co., 1890) and *Lincoln at Work* (Boston: United Society of Christian Endeavor, 1900).

5. William Hayes Ward, ed., *Abraham Lincoln: Tributes from His Associates—Reminiscences of Soldiers, Statesmen and Citizens* (Boston: Thomas Y. Crowell, 1895), p. ix.

6. Ibid., endpapers.

7. During the World War II era, the genre did enjoy a brief renaissance, thanks largely to the efforts of one resolute compiler, Rufus Rockwell Wilson, who published two such collections. See *Intimate Memories of Lincoln* (Elmira, N.Y.: Primavera Press, 1945), and *Lincoln Among His Friends: A Sheaf of Intimate Memories* (Caldwell, Idaho: Caxton Printers, 1942). The field may yet flourish anew. Days before the final manuscript of this book was submitted to the publisher, a charming little collection appeared in print, the first in many years. See Victoria Radford, ed., *Meeting Mr. Lincoln: Firsthand Recollections of Abraham Lincoln by People, Great and Small, Who Met the President* (Chicago: Ivan R. Dee, 1998).

The Abraham Lincoln Papers (microfilm), The Library of Congress.

Angle, Paul. *A Portrait of Abraham Lincoln in Letters by His Oldest Son.* Chicago: The Chicago Historical Society, 1968.

Arnold, Isaac N. *Sketch of the Life of Abraham Lincoln.* New York: John B. Bachelder, 1869.

———. *The Life of Abraham Lincoln.* New York: John B. Bachelder, 1869.

Basler, Roy P., ed. *The Collected Works of Abraham Lincoln,* 9 vols. New Brunswick, N.J.: Rutgers University Press, 1953–55.

Bates, David Homer. *Lincoln in the Telegraph Office: Recollections of the United States Military Telegraph Corps during the Civil War.* New York: Century Co., 1907.

Bayne, Julia Taft. *Tad Lincoln's Father.* Boston: Little, Brown & Co., 1931.

Brooks, Noah. "Personal Recollections of Abraham Lincoln." *Harper's New Monthly Magazine* 31 (July 1865).

———. *Abraham Lincoln.* Washington: National Tribune, 1888.

Burlingame, Michael. *Lincoln Observed: Civil War Dispatches of Noah Brooks.* Baltimore: Johns Hopkins University Press, 1998.

———. *The Inner Life of Abraham Lincoln.* Urbana: University of Illinois Press, 1994.

Carpenter, Francis B. "Anecdotes and Reminiscences of Abraham Lincoln," in Henry J. Raymond. *The Life and Public Services of Abraham Lincoln.* New York: Derby & Miller, 1865.

———. *Six Months at the White House: The Story of a Picture.* New York: Hurd & Houghton, 1866.

Chambrun, Marquis Adolphe de. *Impressions of Lincoln and the Civil War: A Foreigner's Account.* New York: Random House, 1952.

Charney, Theodore S., and Ralph G. Newman, eds. *Artemus Ward on His Visit to Abe Lincoln.* Chicago: The Poor Richard Press, n.d.

Clarke, Asia Booth. "Personal Recollections of Mr. Lincoln." *Scribner's Magazine* 13 (January 1893).

———. *The Unlocked Book: A Memoir of John Wilkes Booth by His Sister.* New York: G. P. Putnam's Sons, 1938.

Conwell, Russell H. *Why Lincoln Laughed.* New York: Harper Bros., 1922.

Dana, Charles A. *Recollections of the Civil War: With the Leaders at Washington and in the Field in the Sixties.* New York: D. Appleton & Co., 1898.

Dennett, Tyler, ed. *Lincoln and the Civil War in the Diaries and Letters of John Hay.* New York: Dodd, Mead & Co., 1939.

Dicey, Edward. *Six Months in the Federal States.* London: Alexander Macmillan, 1863.

———. "Washington during the War." *Macmillan's Magazine* 6 (May 1862).

Douglass, Frederick. *Life and Times of Frederick Douglass, Written by Himself.* Hartford, Conn.: Park Publishing Co., 1881.

Fehrenbacher, Don E., and Virginia Fehrenbacher. *Recollected Words of Lincoln.* Stanford, Calif.: Stanford University Press, 1996.

Fields, Annie, ed. *Life and Letters of Harriet Beecher Stowe.* Boston: Houghton Miflin & Co., 1897.

Franklin, John Hope. *Race and History: Selected Essays, 1838–1988.* Baton Rouge: Louisiana State University Press, 1989.

Franklin, John Hope, and Alfred A. Moss. *From Slavery to Freedom: A History of African Americans,* 7th ed. New York: Alfred A. Knopf, 1994.

Gates, Henry Louis, ed. *Frederick Douglass: Autobiographies.* New York: The Library of America, 1994.

Gerry, Margarita Spalding, ed. *Through Five Administrations: Reminiscences of Colonel William H. Crook, Body-Guard to President Lincoln.* New York: Harper & Bros., 1910.

Grant, Ulysses S. *Personal Memoirs,* 2 vols. New York: Charles L. Webster & Co., 1885–86.

Greeley, Horace. "Greeley's Estimate of Lincoln: An Unpublished Address by Horace Greeley." *Century Magazine* 41 (July 1891).

———. *Recollections of a Busy Life.* New York: J. B. Ford & Co., 1868.

Grimsley, Elizabeth Todd. "Six Months in the White House," *Journal of the Illinois State Historical Society* 19 (October 1926–January 1927).

Hamilton, Charles, and Lloyd Ostendorf. *Lincoln in Photographs: An Album of Every Known Pose.* Norman: University of Oklahoma Press, 1963.

Hammond, Lavern M. "Lincoln's Particular Friend," in Donald F. Tingley, ed. *Essays in Illinois History in Honor of Glenn Huron Seymour*. Carbondale: Southern Illinois University Press, 1968.

Hauranne, Ernest Duvergier de. *A Frenchman in Lincoln's America*. Chicago: R. R. Donnelley & Sons, 1975.

Hawthorne, Nathaniel. "Chiefly About War Matters." *Atlantic Monthly* 10 (July 1862).

Holzer, Harold. *The Lincoln-Douglas Debates: The First Complete, Unexpurgated Text*. New York: HarperCollins, 1993.

Howe, M. A. de Wolfe. *The Life and Letters of George Bancroft,* 2 vols. New York: Charles Scribner's Sons, 1908.

Johannsen, Robert W. *Stephen A. Douglas*. New York: Oxford University Press, 1973.

Jones, Thomas D. *Memories of Lincoln*. New York: Press of the Pioneers, 1934.

Keckley, Elizabeth. *Behind the Scenes, or, Thirty Years a Slave, and Four Years in the White House*. New York: G. W. Carleton & Co., 1868.

Kincaid, Robert L. "Joshua Fry Speed, 1814–1882: Abraham Lincoln's Most Intimate Friend." *Filson Club History Quarterly* 17 (April 1943).

Knight, Henry W. "Personal Recollections of Abraham Lincoln." *The Independent* (4 April 1865).

Lamon, Ward H. *The Life of Abraham Lincoln from His Birth to His Inauguration as President*. Boston: James Osgood & Co., 1872.

Littlefield, John H. Autograph "statement" in the collection of the New-York Historical Society.

Mabee, Carleton. "Sojourner Truth and President Lincoln." *New England Quarterly* 61 (1988).

McPherson, James M. *Battle Cry of Freedom: The Civil War Era*. New York: Oxford University Press, 1988.

———. *The Negro's Civil War: How American Negroes Felt and Acted during the War for the Union*. Urbana: University of Illinois Press, 1982.

Miers, Earl Schenck, ed. *Lincoln Day by Day: A Chronology, 1809–1865,* 3 vols. Washington: Lincoln Sesquicentennial Commission, 1960.

Miller, Edwin Havilland. *Salem is My Dwelling Place: A Life of Nathaniel Hawthorne*. Iowa City: University of Iowa Press, 1991.

Mitgang, Herbert, ed. *Edward Dicey's Spectator of America*. Chicago: Quadrangle Books, 1971.

———, ed. *Lincoln as They Saw Him*. New York: Rinehart & Co., 1956.

Neely, Mark E., Jr. *The Abraham Lincoln Encyclopedia*. New York: McGraw-Hill, 1983.

Neely, Mark E., Jr., and Harold Holzer. *The Lincoln Family Album: Photographs from the Personal Collection of a Historic American Family*. New York: Doubleday, 1990.

Nicolay, John G., and John Hay. *Abraham Lincoln: A History,* 10 vols. New York: Century Co., 1890.

Niven, John, ed. *The Salmon P. Chase Papers. Vol. 1, Journals, 1829–1972*. Kent, Ohio: Kent State University Press, 1993.

Oates, Stephen B. *With Malice toward None: The Life of Abraham Lincoln*. New York: Harper & Row, 1972.

Oldroyd, Osborn H. *The Lincoln Memorial: Album-Immortelles. Original Life Pictures, with Autographs, from the Hands and Hearts of Eminent Americans and Europeans, Contemporaries of the Great Martyr to Liberty, Abraham Lincoln*. New York: G. W. Carleton & Co., 1882.

Paulin, Charles Oscar. "Hawthorne and Lincoln," *American Illustrated* 4 (November 1909).

Randall, Ruth Painter. *Lincoln's Sons*. Boston: Little, Brown & Co., 1955.

Rankin, Henry B. *Intimate Character Sketches of Abraham Lincoln*. Philadelphia: J. B. Lipincott Co., 1924.

———. *Personal Recollections of Abraham Lincoln*. New York: G. P. Putnam's Sons, 1916.

Rhodehamel, John, and Louise Taper, eds. *"Right or Wrong, God Judge Me": The Writings of John Wilkes Booth*. Urbana: University of Illinois Press, 1997.

Russell, William Howard. *My Journal North and South,* 2 vols. London: Bradburn & Evans, 1863.

Sandburg, Carl, and Frederick Hill Meserve. *The Photographs of Abraham Lincoln*. New York: Harcourt, Brace & Co., 1944.

Schurz, Carl. *The Autobiography of Carl Schurz,* 3 vols. New York: McClure & Co., 1907.

Sears, Stephen, ed. *The Civil War Papers of George B. McClellan: Selected Correspondence, 1860–1865*. New York: Ticknor & Fields, 1989.

Sherman, William T. *Memoirs of General William T. Sherman, by Himself,* 2 vols. New York: D. Appleton & Co., 1875.

Simon, John Y., ed. *The Papers of Ulysses S. Grant,* 22 vols. to date. Carbondale: Southern Illinois University Press, 1967–98.

Sparks, Edwin Erle. *The Lincoln-Douglas Debates of 1858.* Collections of the Illinois State Historical Society. Vol. 3, Lincoln Series. Springfield: Illinois State Historical Library, 1908.

Speed, Joshua Fry. "Abraham Lincoln." Lecture, privately printed, 1884.

Staudenraus, P. J. *Mr. Lincoln's Washington: The Civil War Dispatches of Noah Brooks.* New York: Thomas Yoseloff, 1967.

Stoddard, William O. *Abraham Lincoln: The True Story of a Great Life.* New York: Fords, Howard, & Hulbert, 1884.

———. *Inside the White House in War Times.* New York: Charles L. Webster & Co., 1890.

———. *Lincoln at Work: Sketches from Life.* Boston and Chicago: United Society of Christian Endeavor, 1900.

Stoddard, William O., Jr. *Lincoln's Third Secretary: The Memoirs of William O. Stoddard.* New York: Exposition Press, 1955.

Stowe, Harriet Beecher. "Abraham Lincoln," *Littell's Living Age* 80 (6 February 1864).

Strozier, Charles B. *Lincoln's Quest for Union: Public and Private Meanings.* New York: Basic Books, 1982.

Teillard, Dorothy Lamon, ed. *Recollections of Abraham Lincoln, 1847–1865.* Washington, privately printed, 1911.

Temple, Wayne C. "Lincoln as Seen by T. D. Jones," *Illinois Libraries* 58 (June 1976).

Thomas, Benjamin P. *Three Years with Grant, as Recalled by War Correspondent Sylvanus Cadwallader.* New York: Alfred A. Knopf, 1955.

Truth, Sojourner. Letter to Oliver Johnson, 17 November 1864, printed in the *National Anti-Slavery Standard* (17 December 1864); and recollection to Lucy Colman, in the *Sacramento Union* (14 December 1864).

Turner, Justin G., and Linda Levitt Turner. *Mary Todd Lincoln: Her Life and Letters.* New York: Alfred A. Knopf, 1972.

Van Doren, Mark, ed. *The Portable Walt Whitman.* New York: Viking Press, 1974.

Viele, Egbert. "A Trip with Lincoln, Chase, and Stanton," *Scribner's Monthly* 16 (October 1878).

Villard, Harold G., and Oswald Garrison Villard, eds. *Lincoln on the Eve of '61: A Journalist's Story by Henry Villard*. New York: Alfred A. Knopf, 1941.

Villard, Henry. *Memoirs of Henry Villard, Journalist and Financier, 1835–1900*, 2 vols. Boston: Houghton, Mifflin & Co., 1904.

Volk, Leonard Wells. "The Lincoln Life-Mask and How It Was Made," *Century Magazine* 23 (December 1881).

Ward, William Hayes. *Abraham Lincoln: Tributes from His Associates*. New York: Thomas Y. Crowell, 1895.

Warren, Louis A. "Littlefield's Engraving of Lincoln." *Lincoln Lore* No. 592 (12 August 1940).

White, Horace. "Abraham Lincoln." *Putnam's Magazine* (February 1909).

Whitney, Henry Clay. *Life on the Circuit with Lincoln*. Boston: Estes & Lauriat, 1892.

Williams, T. Harry. *Lincoln and His Generals*. New York: Alfred A. Knopf, 1952.

Wilson, Douglas. *Honor's Voice: The Transformation of Abraham Lincoln*. New York: Alfred A. Knopf, 1998.

Wilson, Douglas, and Rodney O. Davis. *Lincoln's Informants: Letters, Interviews, and Statements about Abraham Lincoln*. Urbana: University of Illinois Press, 1998.

Wilson, Edmund. *Patriotic Gore: Studies in the Literature of the American Civil War*. New York: Oxford University Press, 1962.

Wilson, Rufus Rockwell. *Lincoln among His Friends*. Caldwell, Idaho: Caxton Printers, 1942.

Woodson, Thomas et al. *The Centenary Edition of the Works of Nathaniel Hawthorne*. Vol. 18, *The Letters, 1857–1864*. Columbus: Ohio State University Press.

Zall, P. M. *Abe Lincoln Laughing*. Berkeley: University of California Press, 1982.

ACKNOWLEDGMENTS

The Lincoln research trail is a long and demanding one, and one cannot hope to negotiate it without the help of expert guides. Fortunately, I have been blessed with the invaluable assistance of friends and associates from around the country, without whom the task of rediscovering, reevaluating, and reprinting this core of Lincoln recollection would have been impossible.

Thank goodness for the files of the Lincoln Museum in Fort Wayne. Gerald K. Prokopowicz, its resident Historian and Director of Public Programs, has been a patient, amiable, and knowledgeable guide over the years and has been responsive to inquiries made in person, by phone, by facsimile, or by e-mail. I am grateful to him, and to the entire museum staff, including Director Joan Flinspach, who always extends the welcome mat, curator Carolyn Texley and registrar Cindy Van Horn, who know just where the material is and how to get it.

In confessing that my research for this book goes back many years, to the time it was more a concept than a project, I must also acknowledge the help of an earlier generation of Lincoln Museum staff, principally my good friend Mark E. Neely, Jr., then its director and now the McCabe-Greer Professor of Civil War History at the Pennsylvania State University. Ruth Cook, his able assistant in his Fort Wayne days, routinely found files, copied them, and dispatched them with friendly efficiency.

I thank, too, Kim Bauer, curator of the Henry Horner Lincoln Collection at the Illinois State Historical Library in Springfield, and Thomas F. Schwartz, Illinois State Historian, who gave me the time and freedom to wade through files at the museum inside the Old State Capitol in Lincoln's hometown, and then maintained a crucial correspondence of follow-up xerox copies.

Charles Hubbard, Dean of Lincolniana at the Abraham Lincoln Museum at Lincoln Memorial University, has also been helpful and encouraging. So has John Sellers at the Library of Congress. People in the superb photoduplication division at the Library of Congress were also most helpful, particularly the irreplaceable Deborah Evans. At the University of Chicago Library, I had the assistance of university archivist Daniel Meyer, and Debra Levine of the Department of Special Collections. And I am grateful as well to the staff of the New York Public Library main branch on Fifth Avenue and 42nd Street in Manhattan, who never failed to deliver books promptly, even in the midst of reconstruction and renovation; I wish I knew by name each of the indefatigable people who provide such superb reader service.

I wish to acknowledge William Hanchett, the leading scholar of the Lincoln assassination, who went out of his way to locate, copy, and dispatch documents from California, an act of generosity from this senior scholar that touched me deeply. And I thank my friend Eleanor Stoddard, granddaughter of one of Lincoln's private secretaries, William Osborn Stoddard, for sharing so much material so graciously.

David Herbert Donald, the great historian of the Civil War era, was kind enough to nudge me into the high-tech age regarding Lincoln research. I may not quite be up to speed yet, but I would still be languishing in the dark ages had it not been for Professor Donald. I owe a debt, too, to Paul M. Zall, research scholar at the Huntington Library in San Marino, California, who provided sound advice in the field over which he reigns: Lincoln's humor.

And Virginia Fehrenbacher, whose late husband, Don, was one of my idols among Lincoln historians, was kind enough to unearth and copy several elusive, crucial documents at the library at Stanford University. Her effort is deeply appreciated.

I am also indebted to those who provided permission to adapt recollections for this book. Not all of the material that was requested appears on these pages, but not for want of the gracious intervention of people like LeRoy A. Fladseth of Lansing, Michigan, keeper of the flame of one of Lincoln's guards, Seth Stimmel.

My friend Frank J. Williams read the manuscript and made valuable suggestions. Earlier, he again made the resources of his own vast library of Lincolniana available to me. On one memorable occasion he worked patiently with me around a cleanup necessitated by a distracting and distressing flood, checking card catalogs, fetching books and pamphlets, and copying them for my use. As always, this busy jurist and inexhaustible Lincoln scholar and organizer never refused a request for a loaned book, a document, a Xerox copy, or a reel of microfilm. And on three occasions during the period I worked on assembling the entries for this collection, Frank and his wife, Virginia, also welcomed the Holzers to their guesthouse, provided gourmet meals and fine wines, and even locked up their Dobermans. Who could imagine better hosts?

Two people believed in this project from its inception and helped nourish it when it seemed for a time in danger, as Lincoln might have put it, of "winking out." I thank my determined agent, Geri Thoma, and my editor, Amy Gash, for crucial encouragement and valuable guidance.

Edith, my wife of twenty-eight years, probably deluded herself into believing that with our older daughter now living on her own, and the younger attending college, we would have more time than ever for leisure pursuits and each other. If she has minded terribly sharing this stage of our lives with Abraham Lincoln, she has been nice enough not to dwell on it, and I thank her for her support (not to mention her inspiration). As for the children, Meg was always there, school permitting, to accompany us on the research trips to Illinois, Kentucky, Indiana, and Washington, and heroically proofread the entire book; while Remy edited copy with great skill and much sensitivity.

Edith, Meg, and I enjoyed an almost transcendent experience toward the end of the preparation of this book. I had edited a preliminary draft on an eleven-hour plane ride to Israel in the summer of 1998. Then, shortly after our arrival, on our first-ever stroll in Jerusalem, we chanced almost immediately on an intersection we had not known even existed: the corner of King David Street and Abraham Lincoln Street. Here, where civilization virtually began, was reaffirmation that the pursuit of Lincoln remained important. I'm so grateful that it has always been so with my entire family.

Finally, I want to extend special thanks to two exceptional people who have slaved over their keyboards to ready this book for publication. I could not have assembled this volume without my former administrative assistants, now my expert manuscript typists, Amy Varney-Kiet and Re Becca Ames. Had Whitman, Hawthorne, Stowe, and the others represented in this book enjoyed the services of such professionals in their own time, they might have had the freedom to write even more about Abraham Lincoln. But then, this book might have been double the size, required double the typing, needed double the acknowledgments. . . .

Harold Holzer
Rye, New York

LINCOLN ILLUSTRATIONS

(all are details)

Page 1
Photograph by the Mathew Brady Gallery, Washington, February 9, 1864.

Page 11
Composite Lithograph of *President Lincoln and Family Circle* by Joseph Hoover, Philadelphia, 1865.

Page 35
Photograph of Lincoln as Republican nominee for president by William Marsh, Springfield, Illinois, May 20, 1860.

Page 57
Photograph of Lincoln as lawyer-politician by an unknown cameraman, probably Springfield, Illinois, ca. 1859–1860.

Page 83
Comic etching of Lincoln as Don Quixote (with General Benjamin Butler as Sancho Panza) by Adalbert Johann Volck, Baltimore, ca. 1862.

Page 113
Photograph of Lincoln as president-elect by Alexander Gardner, Washington, February 24, 1861.

Page 131
Photograph of Lincoln during his first months as president by an unknown cameraman, Washington, probably June 1861.

Page 145
Photograph of Lincoln as commander in chief with General George B. McClellan (facing him) and his Army of the Potomac staff by Alexander Gardner, near Antietam, Maryland, October 3, 1862.

Page 163
Photograph of Lincoln shortly before his fifty-fifth birthday by the Mathew Brady Gallery, Washington, February 9, 1864.

Page 181
Plaster bust of Lincoln from life by Thomas D. Jones, Springfield, January 1861.

Page 197
The last studio photograph of Lincoln, by Alexander Gardner, Washington, February 5, 1865.

Page 211
Last photograph of Lincoln, by Henry F. Warren, the White House, Washington, March 6, 1865.

PHOTOGRAPH AND ILLUSTRATION CREDITS

(all are details)

Chicago Historical Society, John Carbott, 46 (ref. #ICHi-09427), 183 (ref. #ICHi-12759)

Corbis/Bettmann, 53, 123

Harold Holzer, 78, 83, 181, 211

Library of Congress, 29, 35, 109, 158, 171, 197

The Lincoln Museum, Fort Wayne, Indiana, 1 (ref. #O-89), 11 (ref. #2248), 13 (ref. #4396), 24 (ref. #4009), 27 (ref. #3824), 49 (ref. #58), 57 (ref. #O-15), 66 (ref. #1638), 96 (ref. #3512), 113 (ref. #O-50), 131 (ref. #O-55), 133 (ref. #1310), 135 (ref. #65), 141 (ref. #3179), 145 (ref. #O-62), 154 (ref. #4125), 163 (ref. #O-92), 177 (ref. #1941), 192 (ref. #1341), 198 (ref. #4324), 202 (ref. #1380), 213 (ref. #0-76), 220 (ref. #4517), 229 (ref. #4282), 237 (ref. #2195)

National Portrait Gallery, Smithsonian Institution, Mathew Brady, 165

INDEX